Blackbird Comes Calling

The intersection
of
Faith,
Science and
Depression.

Christians do get depressed.

JACKIE SWANSON

WESTBOW
PRESS
A DIVISION OF THOMAS NELSON

Scripture taken from the New Revised Standard Version Bible, copyright 1989, Division of Christian Education of the National Council of the Churches of Christ in the United States of America. Used by permission. All rights reserved.

WestBow Press books may be ordered through booksellers or by contacting:

WestBow Press
A Division of Thomas Nelson
1663 Liberty Drive
Bloomington, IN 47403
www.westbowpress.com
1-(866) 928-1240

Because of the dynamic nature of the Internet, any web addresses or links contained in this book may have changed since publication and may no longer be valid. The views expressed in this work are solely those of the author and do not necessarily reflect the views of the publisher, and the publisher hereby disclaims any responsibility for them.

Any people depicted in stock imagery provided by Thinkstock are models, and such images are being used for illustrative purposes only.

Certain stock imagery © Thinkstock.

ISBN: 978-1-4497-3416-9 (hc)
ISBN: 978-1-4497-3414-5 (sc)
ISBN: 978-1-4497-3415-2 (e)
Library of Congress Control Number: 2011962431

Printed in the United States of America

WestBow Press rev. date: 1/03/2012

Contents

Part 7

Part 8

Part 9

Dedicated to my husband, Rich

Forward

November 28, 2011

Beloved child of God, you will find a bit of yourself in this book. You may not want to find yourself in these pages, because it means that either you have suffered from depression, or you may know and love someone who has suffered from depression.

In my case, both apply. So, listening to Jackie's voice in this writing brings up many feelings, both good and bad. I find myself in the ups and downs of this illness and in the ups and downs of being a friend/family member/pastor; sometimes helpful and sometimes just plain un-helpful to a brother or sister in Christ who struggles with depression.

If you do or ever have struggled with depression, it is my dearest hope that as you read Jackie's writing, you will be strengthened; strengthened to help yourself (remember the airline instructions—place the oxygen mask over your own face before helping those around you), and strengthened to seek the spiritual and medical help you need.

Jackie provides practical help and personal observation about life with depression. But, best of all, she brings faith in God into the realm of depression. By doing this, she creates a space and a place for you to be both a disciple of Jesus Christ and a person who is ill with depression.

Throughout the pages of "Blackbird Comes Calling", my dear friend has fearlessly told the story of her own experience of depression; sharing with you some frightening times. But she has also shared her deep faith in God's love, grace and mercy—in spite of the illness. She tells how faith held her together during hard times. She is telling you the truth. I know this because I have seen her during some of those darkest of days. Even then, when her depression was at its worst, she believed in the love of God shown to us through the life, death and resurrection of Jesus Christ.

Jackie's writing style in this book reflects the journey; sometimes a brief focus on one small, profound thought, at other times a more expansive look at a particular issue, at yet another time a pulpit-worthy message of the Gospel. Each piece commendable of consideration and reflection.

So, beloved child of God, read on. May you find hope and encouragement for your own journey.

Mary Lou Aune
Child of God and friend of the author

Part 1

1

The Resurrection of Jesus Christ

"I say to the Lord, 'You are my Lord; I have no good apart from you'" (Psalm 16:2).

What would life look like without the resurrection of Jesus Christ? It would be empty and without content; there would be nothingness and an absolute void. Take out the resurrection, and there is nothing left—nothing at all. We know there was the resurrection of Jesus Christ; without it, we would not be alive today. God raises the dead, and the resurrection is a continuous action in that life-giving process. The resurrection did not just happen once; it happens every day.

If there is no resurrection, our lives have no meaning whatsoever—but Christ did rise from the dead. Jesus was killed, put in a tomb for three days, and lived again so that you can live again—and yes, you will live again. It is essential for us to know this and to believe this, for without the resurrection, there is nothing—nothing at all. Your life is of value. You have life because of who Christ is and what Christ did—*live.*

2

More Than a Mood Swing

"Save me, O God, for the waters have come up to my neck" (Psalm 96:1).

This writing is about major depression as I have lived it, which is at the point where faith and science coexist. This is a compilation of my personal journey of years with depression weaved together with my faith journey and my rejoicing in the expertise of the medical profession. Inspired and written specifically for people with depression, this is appropriate for all people, especially friends or family of the depressed, clergy, church workers, doctors, and therapists. This is a Christian writing mainly compiled for my many brothers and sisters I don't know who struggle with depression.

The term *depression* can be confusing, since it is often used to describe normal emotional reactions. At the same time, it is hard to recognize, because its symptoms can resemble other illnesses. I can look back now and realize multiple times throughout my life I had undiagnosed depression. Some of the diagnoses I received were flu, too much stress, lack of sleep, hypertension, improper eating, premenstrual syndrome, and just a normal reaction to a recent loss or change. The only time in those first years I was legitimately diagnosed as depressed was due to a normal acute reaction to a life event—a miscarriage. The treatment, however, did not match the severity of the illness.

A miscarriage had recently put me in the hospital for a couple of days, and now that I was home, we needed groceries. Not really feeling up to it, I went to the store anyway. It was a fairly large market, and I started pushing the grocery cart around. This was my usual shopping spot, so I knew where everything was located and thought, "*this won't take long.*" I got lost in the store. My memory didn't work. The list I had made seemed like gobbledygook. It featured the usual grocery store abbreviations: OJ, TP, choc, hmb—they all meant nothing to me. So I went about finding what I could decipher—bananas, milk, bread—and I wandered around the store, not knowing where anything was located, occasionally spotting something from my list and putting it in the cart.

I do remember coming into the store around 8:00 a.m. Finally one of the workers came up to me; others were timidly watching from down the aisle. The store employee asked me if I was doing okay. I asked him what time it was; it was 10:30. My comment was that I didn't feel good. He walked me to the cashier, I bought what was in the cart, and I drove home. Upon telling my husband, he insisted I see the doctor, so I set an appointment for the next morning. Our family doctor's comment was, "You have a right to be depressed; look what you have just gone through. Everyone feels sad or discouraged sometimes." This is the first time anyone in the medical profession used the word *depressed* to define what I was living with.

Two weeks later, I was back to the doctor. My not getting over these feelings should have been an indicator to him that something more was going on than a normal response to a loss, but he offered me a tranquilizer and sent me home.

Sadness at loss is normal but can also trigger a major depressive episode. Some years later, I recognized the grocery store incident as more than a normal reaction to a loss. Most major environmental changes—such as job changes, moves, or the birth of a child—can set off some degree of depression. With people prone to major depressive episodes, the depression may become more than a passing thing.

> *Gracious God, help us to see and feel your compassion as*
> *we push through the troubles of life. May the mercy of*
> *Jesus turn our mourning into dancing.*

3

I Never Saw Him Again

"Protect me, O God, for in you I take refuge"
(Psalm 16:1).

Through most of my years, symptoms followed me night and day without end. Good times with our family or happy news gave momentary relief but did not alleviate the symptoms. Often I was so disabled by feelings of despair, I didn't have enough energy to call a doctor—and when I did see a doctor, my symptoms were passed off as something else or were related back to a recent change in my life. It is jolting and scary to realize depression is the illness that underlies the majority of suicides in our country, and I wandered around depressed for years.

In the attempt to prevent my set of circumstances from happening to you, I am compelled to take a good look at depression from the inside out. In my own searching, I have found volumes of literature, books, web pages, and informational sessions on depression. Being a person of faith, I also searched for materials written from a faith perspective to help through a Christian lens but found very little. What I did find along this avenue were authors claiming if you had enough faith, you should be at peace. I totally knew that was not true, for honestly, I am one of the most faithful people I know, and I was definitely suffering with depression.

I find there is a huge disparity between what is known about depression, what we do about depression, and how I experience depression. This writing investigates depression from the angles of science and faith because I find both are essential elements in life to be ability to live with depression and all the set-backs and sadness it brings. The purpose of this writing is to tell how Christ—in and through sound medical care—has helped me live with major depression.

The boss carried in a pile of work marked "Paradigm Shifts" and handed it to the employee, saying, "Here's your work for the day." If only it were that easy to change the paradigm of depression from a hushed mental concern which carries a large stigma to a publicly accepted medical condition—like diabetes, asthma, colitis, or hypertension—people suffering could get the help and consideration they need. If someone brings up the word *depression,* it leaves us standoffish and reluctant to get involved. The epidemic of depression is upon us, and it will affect us one way or another.

ScienceDaily (July 25, 2011)—Depression affects 121 million people worldwide. It can affect a person's ability to work, form relationships, and destroy quality of life. At its most severe depression can lead to suicide and is responsible for 850,000 deaths every year. A question of legitimate concern is, "How's your depression today?"

Depression knows no boundaries and has no shame. Depression attacks, slithers, and destroys lives wherever it can. It is a prevalent illness making demands on minds, bodies, and souls. The symptoms are numerous, and it lingers in all professions, races, socioeconomic planes, climates, and continents.

My first job out of college was in a large bank in the Midwest. It was an exciting time in banking, for automation was expanding the banking industry. One man, who was a major player in this, was especially bright and exciting to watch as he exploded with joy with each new discovery. He was very competent, smiling, bouncy, thrilled with his job, and a joy to work around. He was well-known among the bank employees, and he always showed interest in other people.

One day, he didn't show up for work, and this was totally out of character. He most certainly would call or notify someone if he was delayed. Later in the day, rumor had it he had a nervous breakdown. I never saw him again. There was no group collection for a gift; no one reported going to see him or talking to him. He truly became a common-day leaper. Thirty years later, I was encouraged to resign because I too was having emotional problems—a nervous breakdown, if you will. And I too never saw any of my colleagues again—there was no group card, no one called, and no one came to see me. I truly became a common-day leaper.

The term *nervous breakdown* is no longer part of the professional mental health language, but it seems to carry a common-knowledge vision of a person who has really fallen off the edge. This lack of public education about mental health complicates the issue of having mental health problems, because few people know what you are talking about. The misunderstandings about major depression run deep. Hopefully this book will offer you some sound support in your life as a person living with depression and will inform others of your malady.

God, keep us steadfast in you all day long.

4

Loss of Employment

"Judge me, O Lord according to my righteousness and
according to the integrity that is in me" (Psalm 7:8b).

The day I gave in to the pressure to resign became a glorious day
of bitterness, resentment, relief, and surrender. Thanks be to God,
it was over—all the months of agony and uncertainty, pushing
and pulling, freezing and melting. With the amount of emotional
turmoil and decomposition, I should not have been climbing behind
the wheel of the car to drive the hour and a half home. I've done
it before—driven when incapacitated from despair and depression.
"I can do this" is my personal cheerleading attempt. Driving is just
one of a million things I have done under the influence of major
depression.

It is easy to know if people recognize my mental status. The
people in the main office where I had just resigned really did know
I was depressed because I don't display it publicly. My mental health
concerns were never a secret during the candidacy process, my years
at seminary, or the year of internship. They have all forgotten. Why
shouldn't they forget? I rarely give physical or outward signs of the
return of depression. I do not give any hints in the public arena. I've
learned through the years to keep it under wraps, because the stigma

is too great. At home, it is a different story. At home, I let my guard down and collapse under the stress. Few have seen the collapsed side of me or known that part of me.

It's hard for people who haven't experienced depression to understand its impact and severity. People treat me differently if they know I have mental health concerns. Some show reluctance, while others want to tend to my every need. Others have a look of awe, as it to ask, "How does she manage?" The answer to that specific question is different with each passing day. Some days are easier than other days.

Through the years, I have lived with or denied the existence of my own major mental health concerns. With Band-Aid approaches from doctors and no real, honest-to-goodness psychological assessment, it was years before I had official diagnoses.

Lord, in your life, you taught us how to live and pray and offered us hope. Help us to continue in this hope.

5

Shall We Gather at the River?

"For you, O Lord, are my hope, my trust, O Lord, from my youth. Upon you I have leaned from my birth; it was you who took me from my mother's womb. My praise is continually of you" (Psalm 71:5-6).

We live in an old creamery situated on the north bank of the Winnebago River. It was built in 1900, and as the story goes, it made the creamiest butter ever eaten. An old man name Virgil up at the café brought a picture to show me of half a dozen men standing outside the creamery, all in a line, covered in wader boots and long white aprons—a butter-maker's garb. Virgil pointed out one man in the picture and said it was him years ago—back when he was a kid. If you are not sure what a creamery is, it is where the dairy farmers brought their milk for processing. The milk was separated out (the cream settles to the top), and other dairy products were made from it, such as butter and cheese. This particular creamery is even made from local bricks manufactured at a long-gone brick factory down river. Since its creamery days, the building has also been a steakhouse, and at one time, it served as a tea house. We bought it when the tea house was closing business. We didn't have a business to run there; we bought the creamery to live in.

The creamery is a unique place to live—charming, quaint, and somewhat mysterious. It has a beautiful yard with early spring fragrant lily of the valley and purple hibiscus, red-orange poppies and rows of dancing daisies. A variety of hosta stationed around the yard seem to stand guard to the many doings in the yard. All year, day lilies, iris, or fancy grasses adorn the yard that runs right to the bank of the river. The entire setting is serene and pastoral, ever reminding me of the 23rd Psalm.

I do believe we came to the creamery in the first place on the prodding of the Holy Spirit—at least, the Spirit was pushing me into it; this was not so with the rest of my family. Over the twelve years here, we have experienced, suffered, rejoiced, and faced much human happiness, sadness, devastation, and trauma. The whole of our lives at the creamery represents life and emotions beyond our control. Out of the life lived, cherished, and survived during the creamery years, Jesus was my mainstay.

In some mental health circles, religious ritual is a symptom of mental health concerns. I must say, my over-the-board delving into religion certainly could have been a symptom; I just found it comforting and necessary to get through my days. Christ has always been with me, so it wasn't a new thing for me to spend time reading; writing; praying; meditating; wandering by the river, deep in reflection; or taking retreats to quiet places. Does religion make mental health healthier, or does religion serve as a diversion to the issues of the day? In my experience, religions does both, and I'm really not sure that it makes a difference—or for that matter, a definitive study

In the 1950s, I grew up in the Midwest on the farm. I was baptized at a little rural Lutheran church soon after my birth. From this church life came my sense of belonging, for the people were my friends, my group, and my home. I was always accepted in this safe place that afforded me the chance to individuate as my own independent child of God. I knew this to be true, because I had a glow-in-the-dark cross tied to the end of the string on my pull light, and it indeed continuously glowed with the light of God.

If you have ever seen or heard about the Lutheran Church Basement Ladies of the 1960s, it describes my young years of observing the mothers and grandmothers. The lutefisk dinners complete with rutabagas, lefsa, krumkake, and egg coffee were annual events involving every living soul in the congregation. This is when I first watched a man, elbow-deep in soap suds, washing out a huge potato pot. He held a special place in my heart from that day forward, for he did this with purpose and calm, accepting his role as one among many. My church family taught me trust, self-respect, and personal peace. By the age of thirteen, I was graciously accepted as the church pianist. During my young years, I knew two pastors, both of whom had positive impacts on me. They both demonstrated family values, personal piety, and global mission. Luther League (the youth group) was amazing, along with summer Bible camps. And my confirmation classmates and I studied our confirmation studies diligently—not just to get through, but to make our church family proud and learn what was vitally important, because this knowledge was vitally important to each one of us.

In the 1960s, the sacrament of communion was realized after the rite of confirmation. I'm not sure why, but it worked wonders for me in my own faith. Our Lutheran church was very God-oriented and Jesus-centered; the Holy Spirit was important but not spoken about as much as the other two persons of the trinity. However, with the bread and wine, the Holy Spirit became my new friend. A new relationship was born, and I truly felt the Holy Spirit honored my place in the kingdom of God. I in turn honored the Holy Spirit's unique person of the trinity.

These formative years were the foundation for my college years from 1970-1974, where I studied music, religion, and psychology. My husband and I met at college.

The rite of marriage brought home the life of love. The love my husband and I had for each other only gave us a glimpse of the divine love God had for us. We found that through God, we became yet another element and were able to hope together. Marriage exemplified forgiveness and strengthened trust. Marriage was an emotional time, and with each of our own firm foundations in the church, we were able to be safe together and explore our individual and married lives. Marriage brought clarity. It helped define our firm foundation in Christ as a married couple, as parents, and later as grandparents.

My husband and I were married for thirty-six years. He died suddenly on May 26, 2010 at the age of fifty-seven. We raised two daughters during the historic time of the merger between the ALC (American Lutheran Church) and LCA (Lutheran Church in America). Along with the merger came the need for a comprehensive new hymnal, and through a joint effort, the red hymnal became the green hymnal. All this collaboration was amazing to me because of the denominations' ability to actually work together for a common goal. During the 1980s, our family helped at church in any way needed—playing music, teaching, ushering, serving as committee members, and the like.

Through a life of faith, we have choices. Learning to make loving choices becomes a life-long commitment. Learning to surrender my personal will to the divine will is a daily discipline. Through the years, as everyone does, I have messed up. God's discipline is sure, but so is God's grace. With a lifetime of faith and love for God, the journey tends to get more difficult as God challenges us to grow, and at times, this road is very rocky. It does not dissuade me but reinforces in me that God travels with me, leading me on the path, where I am sure-footed.

Our family struggles were not unusual. We lost some pregnancies, my husband had some major medical problems along the way, our youngest daughter struggled with the world of drugs her teenage years, our older daughter declared her commitment to another woman, and my husband and I lost three parents. There were challenges to face with jobs and money, houses and cars, and daily life's demands. Our strong hold was always God and the shield of God's protection.

All I ever wanted to do was to work in God's church. I wanted the reverence, universal love, and time to seek the truth through devoted service. My main interest of study was religion in preparation for seminary. The first women were just beginning to be seminary-educated and ordained into the church. However, the timing was wrong for me. My husband and I visited a seminary and considered the financial ramifications of my continued education and decided we just were not ready. After a career of more than twenty years in nursing, I went to seminary.

The years from 1999-2003 were the most expansive of my life. I couldn't get enough studies, and the new friendships were etched in granite. While I moved through the seminary with the entrance interview, endorsement interview, CPE (clinical pastoral education), and approval interview, my health started to deteriorate. It seemed the closer I got to God, the harder the demons worked to hurt me.Seminary became an emotional and mental struggle, and depression took hold. My studies stayed strong, the professors were supportive and pastoral, and my family and friends encouraged and cared for me as I needed.

I graduated from seminary in May of 2003—one week after my husband had surgery to remove a cancerous kidney. My first call started in June of 2003, and I was ordained on Pentecost Sunday in 2003. The place to which I was called was a wonderful blend of two churches—one country maternal/paternal farming congregation and an i—town church comprised of a mix of workers and families. The timing couldn't have been worse. With a combined accumulation of events, the members of in-town church and I did not hit it off. Only a partial working relationship developed, and there were some wonderful moments there; however, for the most part, the relationship was tense. The country church members and I bonded early on and found mutual trust and care for each other. Within six months, my health started to deteriorate again, rendering me incapable of sound decisions. In December of 2004, after nineteen months, I resigned. Now after six years, my health is much better, thought I experience occasional set-backs.

Self-actualization—the spiritual connection in the present; a complete, selfless unity with God—came early for me in my twenties. I already knew of God speaking to me, listening to me, and answering my prayers. During my twenties, the major depressive episodes started, but it would be many years before I was truly diagnosed and treated for depression. Prior to the diagnoses, my episodes of depression, anxiety, obsessive-compulsive behaviors, angry explosions, and near hysteria were explained away as premenstrual syndrome, the flu, or high blood pressure.

Now I refer to depression as the blackbird that comes calling. It is like a huge blackbird on a still white winter day, moving through the sanctity of a reverent place, cawing and disturbing, jarring and obtrusive. Through the years, I have had bouts of depression. Certainly some had do to with situations such as the loss of pregnancies, the death of parents, and the cancer and death of my husband, and all the accumulative losses we gather over the years. However, I have had two severe bouts of clinical depression—one in 2000 from August through December and another from January of 2005 through June of 2006. As always, God has seen me through by providing the life-saving Christ and the comforting and endearing Holy Spirit. Through fine doctors, therapists, family members, and friends, I have made it through some near-death-producing times. I continue under a doctor's scrutiny and care, including proper medication and talk therapy. I have learned great courage in the face of adversity and have lived in the circle of the triune God.

Life's experiences do have a way of interfering with how we perceive our lives should be! For me, the interface and clarity is found in the world of God. With God being timeless, unwavering, and absolute, I can explore the world, other people, and myself, knowing all these varied relationships exemplify God. God's call to me comes from my early years, my growing-up years, my adult years, and the many people around me. My friends at church challenge me to continue with my spiritual gifts of preaching, teaching, counseling, and caring. God has afforded me awareness of God's daily pulse, and I am excited to answer; however, I have health limitations. What I want to do in my heart and mind is not what my body is capable of doing. The medications make me sluggish and exhausted, the weight gain and hair loss are discouraging, and the need to explain myself becomes burdensome. However, God's faithfulness and guidance has come to me through the church and God's people. God's love and compassion has come to me in the depths of despair. I continue my active life within the church, where God's people hold me close, tend to my wounds, and laugh at my jokes.

During these last twelve years living at the creamery, I have learned some coping skills, written devotions and short essays, created some Bible studies, and gathered many personal prayers. Group worship and small group prayer along with mantras, ostinatos, and reflections have filled many pages in my journals.

I am at a point in my life which is not one I ever envisioned for myself where loneliness is my daily existence and extreme simplicity my preferred lifestyle. I am in a small house now. The creamery is still there by the river; no one lives there now.

God, you always know your children, what we need,
and when we need it. In all our anxiety, give us trusting
and faithful hearts.

6

"You Will Need Therapy the Rest of Your Life"

"I have become like a broken vessel" (Psalm 31:12b).

Through disability with the church I was able to set up two days of out-patient evaluations with the mental health clinic at a large hospital in Minneapolis. A kindly man who sat across the table from me. The lengthy conversation with this gentle man took place late in the morning of the second day of my assessment. Toward the end of our time together, he leaned into my face and slowly said, "You will need therapy the rest of your life." This one fact emptied me of the last drop of hope I had for any normalcy.

"You will need therapy the rest of your life," the doctor said. He did not say "you might need therapy for a few months" or "it would be a good idea if you had therapy." He said, "You will need therapy the rest of your life." This conjures up a picture of me as an old, yellow-haired woman, propped up in a wheelchair, with her head hanging down. Along comes a sharp, young psychologist to ask yet again, "So how's your depression today?"

Lunchtime came, and I needed air. The coordinating psychologist suggested a restaurant within walking distance from the hospital.

"Take your time," he said with a nod. The wind was bitter cold, burning my ears as I walked the two blocks. Just the night before, the newscaster said it hit minus 54 degrees in Ermannus.

The previous night, I had recovered from the first day of assessments by lying on the hotel bed, watching three straight hours of reality TV. The first was about a team of builders who demonstrated how to build a house for a needy family. Then I watched a picture-perfect bachelor show how to narrow down choices for a wife. In the last show, a nanny entered a misfit home run by the children and gave the parents instructions on how to raise their family.

As I found a bagel to eat, I realized the whole country wants to know how to live, and reality TV is the new textbook. All the reality shows were about how to do something—build a house, pick a wife, raise children. Maybe I could offer up a series on how to live with major depressive disorder with psychotic episodes.

As I returned to the psychologist's office, the psychiatrist was just leaving. He offered me these words with a partial smile: "Take good care of yourself." He knew how difficult it would be for me to live these words. As the psychologist and I settled in for another session, he remarked, "Upon looking at the results of your assessment tools, the Taylor Johnson and the MMPI-2, we—the assessment team—are not sure how you are even standing up. And you say you have never been hospitalized? With your profile, Dr. Lowell was sure you were hospitalized. But no?"

The results of the assessments, history-taking, and conversations over the past two days became the diagnostic information used to prepare recommendations for my future ministry. The assessment team recommended six to twelve months of medical disability, an acquired psychologist and a psychiatrist close to my home, and a reliable network of nearby people to respond to my cries for help, complete with a code sheet of words that share my desperation, since my outward demeanor rarely does.

It took a few weeks to get everything into place because of insurance issues and how the company covers therapists. Some patients have a limited number of visits and have restrictions on how many visits they can make in any given time frame. When you are sick, it is hard to figure these things out, so don't be afraid to get help with the leg work. Take care as you follow through on your medical necessities.

Part 2

7

Major Depression

"God reached down from on high and took me;
God drew me out of the mighty waters" (Psalm 18:16).

There is no cure for major depression—only treatment of symptoms. Because major depression is chronic, it leads to the feeling of lack of control. This is why medical treatment is so essential, and in many cases, medications are essential to avoid the feeling of being out of control. For me, the blackbird signifies that the time has really come that my own control is not productive or attainable. This is where I fight the sense of failure, guilt, and inadequacy. The blackbird is so dark and sinister, I find myself in self-imposed isolation in fear of corrupting others with this horrible bird. There was a time I felt I deserved this malady—that misery was the only life for me. The ugly truth was my self-rejection, self-misunderstanding, and a life of compounding problems. God entered, put me in front of the mirror, and said, "I created you; you are good." "Before I formed you in the womb I knew you, and before you were born I consecrated you" (Jeremiah 1:5).

Thank you, God, for creating me and loving me so dearly.
As I live my life, Lord, always point me to the cross and
the empty tomb to give me strength.

8

Medical Care

*"You gave me a wide place for my steps under me, and my
feet did not trip" (Psalm 18:36).*

It is very important to seek out and get proper medical care. It is
necessary to rule out medical pathologies, which only a doctor can
do. If you cannot get yourself to the doctor because you are too
tired, unfocused, or timid to talk about your symptoms, which
depressed people often pass off as temporary sadness, hopefully
you can commit to another person to help you get an appointment
and keep it. If you really cannot bring yourself to do it, try to call
your local mental health clinic or the local hospital to get a reliable
referral.

When I sought help in the 1980s and 1990s, my efforts were met
with limited success; however, the mental health care environment
in the current delivery health system has improved over the years.
The bottom line is to get help; at least try to muster up a phone call
or an impulsive drop-in to a mental health clinic. With a qualified
doctor or psychiatrist, a treatment plan can be established. This
writing is too limited to go into great detail, but there are different
prescribed medications to help relieve some of the symptoms of

depression. Believe me—properly diagnosed and treated depression is literally a lifesaver.

Speaking of life-saving, suicidal thoughts can lead to the real deal. If you are suicidal in thought, call someone—anyone. 911 is also available. With people closest to you (if you haven't pushed them all away), establish some simple codes to alert them to your suicidal thoughts. Often expressions are said with displaced emotion and do not match the gravity of the situation. For example, phrases such as "I'm frozen," "I can't breathe," or "help me" should bring resounding responses from others. However, if your emotional state is bland, which comes with depression, you may not be taken seriously, so it is important to make sure those closest to you understand that regardless of your presenting emotional state, you are extremely serious. If your cries for help are delivered in a calm, exact fashion, you may be overlooked completely, so you must be proactive and alert those closest of words that signal drowning.

As sick as you are, it comes down to this: you are most likely your own and only advocate. Mental health is not an exact science, but do get medical help. Get help before you hurt yourself or anyone else. I stress the importance of entering the mental health care system in some way, for it is imperative to your treatment and hopeful recovery. If you see yourself in this list (which is not exhaustive), seek help.

◆ Noticeable change of appetite (either loss or gain)
◆ Noticeable change in sleeping patterns (sleeping too much, too little, or fitfully)
◆ Loss of interest in pleasurable activities
◆ Loss of energy; fatigue
◆ Feelings of worthlessness

◆ Persistent feelings of hopelessness

◆ Feelings of guilt

◆ Inability to concentrate; indecisiveness

◆ Recurring thoughts of death or suicide; wish to die (seek help immediately!)

◆ Melancholia (overwhelming feelings of sadness and grief), accompanied by waking at least two hours earlier than normal, feeling more depressed in the morning, and moving significantly more slowly

◆ Physical symptoms, such as headaches, stomachaches, constipation, diarrhea, runny nose, or cold sores

Depression is now classified as a medical condition, because it affects the whole body and results in the need for medical treatment. Depression is a medical condition like diabetes, colitis, asthma, or hypertension and needs constant monitoring. In the acute phase of depression, more vigorous care is required. With the diagnoses of Major Depressive Disorder with psychotic episodes, I had reached another new arena of my own mental illness. Adding this to my already established diagnoses of PTSS (post-traumatic stress syndrome), DID (disassociate identity disorder), SAD (seasonal affective disorder), and GAD (generalized anxiety disorder), I was, for the first time in my life, actually feeling some grounding in knowing what my condition had a name. This in itself seemed like a major accomplishment to me.

The difference between depression and an MDD (major depressive disorder) is that MDD symptom cause a significant distress or impairment in social, occupational, or other important areas of functioning (such as difficulty maintaining personal hygiene) and a morbid preoccupation with worthlessness, suicidal ideation, psychotic symptoms, or psychomotor retardation. I also had the added feature of agoraphobia and social phobia. Let me unpack this for you.

First, agoraphobia is defined as anxiety about being in places from which escape might be difficult. Help may not be available in the event of having unexpected panic. For me, agoraphobic fears included being outside our house. There are times being in a group of people, standing in a grocery line, not seeing an immediate exit, or even sitting in a theater between people must be avoided. At my worst, I cannot drive the car. Marked distress sets in with panic, and I require one of two things (or both): I must be home, and I must have someone with me.

For example, one day, while feeling much better, I ventured out in the car with a self-prepared route and a few specific tasks to do. I was to stop at the post office to get the mail, drive ten miles to go tanning (tanning helps with the seasonal affective disorder), drive another six miles to the bookstore to pick up a book I had ordered, and then as a reward, pick up a new chicken ranch sandwich from the sub shop to take home for lunch. Well, I didn't do too badly. I made it to the post office and drove the ten miles to go tanning. After tanning, I got back in the car, and panic set in as a delayed reaction to the tanning bed. I attempted to get it together so I could finish my errands, but I just couldn't do it, so I skipped the drive to the bookstore and the sub sandwich, drove back home in a hurry, jumped out of the car, and made a beeline for the house. Once I was inside, the immediate panic subsided, but the general anxiety persisted for another hour. It helped to call someone on the phone and listen to them talk.

Second is psychosis. The word *psychotic* always sounds so—well, crazy. Major depression, seasonal affective disorder, and even post-traumatic stress sound reasonable to have, but psychosis seems to go to a different level. Medically psychosis is described this way: Delusions, hallucination, and/or a depressive stupor are present with a severe depressive episode. The delusions usually involve ideas of sin, poverty or imminent disasters. Auditory or olfactory hallucinations are usually of defamatory or accusatory voices or of rotting filth or decomposing flesh.

The symptoms of major depressive disorder can develop over days, weeks, or months; yet one case of major depression I suffered came on suddenly, accompanied with many delusions and hallucinations. This episode was from a clinical I was participating in during the summer of 2000. (I will share more about this later.)

It is estimated that 50 to 85 percent of the people who have one major episode will eventually have another episode. Interestingly enough, many people in the northern hemisphere have the regular appearance of symptoms between the beginning of October to the end of November and regular remission from mid-February to mid-April. I have suffered depression every month of the year; however, this aforementioned time frame does seem to lend itself to a more difficult time.

A variety of biological indicators have shown there are significant changes in brain chemistry and an overall reduction in brain activity with Major Depressive Disorder. The very nature of depression alters the way you think and react to situations, generally to the point of profound pessimism because of a general overwhelmingly negative outlook. One major consequence of Major Depressive Disorder is that as the progression worsens, the depression becomes controlling. This is all the more reason to get help early. It is not unusual for depressed persons to damage themselves occupationally, socially, financially, and/or physically.

No specific cause for depression has been identified, but there are a number of factors involved. This is not an exhaustive list.

◆ The tendency to develop depression may be inherited or run in families.
◆ Brain chemicals called *neurotransmitters* allow electrical signals to move from the axon of one nerve cell to the neuron of another nerve cell. A shortage of neurotransmitters impairs brain communication.
◆ Early life experiences such death of a parent, rejection, neglect, or chronic illness may cause depression.
◆ Life experiences such as job loss, financial difficulties, or long-term stress may cause depression.
◆ Certain illnesses may contribute to depression, as can some prescription medications.
◆ Alcohol can have a negative effect on mood.
◆ Depression can occur postpartum.
◆ Living with a depressed person can cause depression.

Treatment of depression varies and is different for each person. Medication prescribed by a psychiatrist may be essential along with psychotherapy. Other alternative and essential treatments I have found are exercise, vitamins, and avoiding certain foods. The effectiveness of treatment also depends on a patient's level of optimism and hope at the time. While treatment is generally effective for me, it is the support of family and friends that truly makes me heal and get well. You may spend years without professional help, self-soothing and coping on your own for a variety of reasons, often for fear of ridicule, embarrassment, or shame. It takes a leap of faith to get the necessary treatment. The people who can help you are a special gift from God. Please seek out help.

> *Good and gracious God, you have blessed us with health*
> *care professionals beyond belief. Please bless each one,*
> *providing them with the training, education, and passion*
> *needed to care for the population of the mentally ill,*
> *remembering always that their gifts are from you.*

9

Dietary Needs

"You . . . will revive me again" (Psalm 71:20).

Three times I have felt so bad, I realized even the foods I was eating caused depression to linger longer or be more intense. My own attempt at finding good food sources and not-so-good food sources led to me creating these charts for myself. They may help you, too. Suggest them to your doctor first and clear any diet changes with the medication you are on. For example, one of my medications restricts my eating of grapefruit. It is also known that increased consumption of dairy products such as milk, cheese, ice cream, and yogurt can be an indicator that depression is coming. Also, depressed people generally consume many dairy products. I don't know if there is a cause and effect, but it is worth checking out.

Some food products which I have found do not bother me at all and are good for me are turmeric, basil, dark chocolate, concord grape juice and jelly, almonds, rice, applesauce, bananas, and tomatoes. What foods do not bring you down is really trial and error. With some time investment over the years, this is the list I have compiled.

First of all, avoid caffeine, MSG, white sugar, white flour, gluten, margarine, and scrupulously avoid fried foods. These particular foods seem to elevate anxiety and case lingering sad moods. One doctor told me to avoid the microwave as well, because it changes the chemical configuration in foods and can leech chemicals from the plate or container the food is in or on.

The following list offers some suggestions on foods nutritionists, doctors and therapists have found are beneficial to maintaining an elevated mood. I too recommend these foods. I am not sure if they actually helped me but they most certainly were not a detriment to my well-being.

Daily consume moderate amounts of green tea, cinnamon, honey, dark chocolate, molasses, basil, turmeric, concord grape juice or jelly. Consume 2-4 servings of apples, oranges, pineapple, cherries, cranberries, papaya, apricots, blackberries, blueberries or strawberries. Consume 2-3 servings of protein a day, such as salmon, whitefish, halibut, eggs, turkey, soy or dried beans. Have 3-5 vegetable servings a day, including tomato, broccoli, beets, spinach, cabbage, carrots, asparagus or pumpkin. Consume 2-3 servings of fat-free dairy and eat breads and whole grains in moderation. Include olive oil in your diet daily too.

Come, Lord Jesus, be our guest, and let this food
to us be blessed.

10

Betrayal

"You show me the path of life" (Psalm 16:11).

Complicating an already very delicate situation can cause feelings of betrayal. I know I have let myself down when obvious symptoms of depression show their ugly heads and I don't seek immediate help. If indeed I know what is going on or what is coming, why not push harder for help? The obvious explanations come in the form of pride and fear; I am too proud to admit trouble is brewing and too afraid to give into it again.

I also feel betrayed by the system of people for not taking better care of me, and I feel betrayed by colleagues who cared about me but inferred they didn't want to get involved in my predicament. When I say this, it appears that I am passing the buck or placing blame, stating "they did it" or "they didn't do it" when in fact it isn't finger-pointing at all. The inability of the system to identify a causality in its midst has been taught to us. Symptoms of depression such as exhaustion, irritability, digestive trouble, and the inability to make decisions, label a person as having poor coping skills. In fact, even though I was within minutes of icing myself, the final report stated my coping skills were inadequate. I totally beg to differ, for if I had not coped the way I had, I would be dead.

I am afraid the church also promotes loyalty to the political system within the church rather than a loyalty to the people that make up the body of Christ. Providing money for world relief or even taking food to the local food pantry becomes the grid by which we assess our help to people. However, the church has gotten so caught up in its own pragmatic system that flesh-and-blood people standing in our midst are pushed to the rear.

Four months a year have five Sundays. These Sundays became a food collection processional offering day. Little kids and grandpas alike proudly came down the center aisle to pile up nonperishable items into a grocery cart. After worship, someone would box up the groceries and take them to the local food pantry. Our task was complete; we had fed the poor. In this same community, a man lived in his car. He parked in secluded areas at night to sleep and drove to certain places during the day where he would find people to talk to and something to eat. He rarely showered, was dirty and grimy, and didn't smell good. On a food collection Sunday, this man came to church and slid into a back pew. As I shook his hand as he left the sanctuary, I invited him for coffee and rolls in the fellowship hall, and absolutely no one sat with him. He ate his roll, drank his coffee, and left to a collective sigh of relief in the fellowship hall.

This demonstrates a taught loyalty to the system. We inadvertently teach our congregations immense loyalty to some peculiar structure while someone in our midst is in over her head, drowning. This is the model by which we gather the faithful; no wonder no one is banging on the church door to get in.

I felt betrayed. I was in the midst of the people. I was in over my head, drowning. However, with mental illness, I too am part of the problem, for I find myself pushing away, denying how sick I am, and refusing to give in. Much of the damage done to me could have been diverted; however, I too had a peculiar loyalty to the very system that was killing me.

Depression is no one's fault. I have tried to make it someone's fault for years. There is always the need to blame something; childhood years, genetic makeup, the moon, milk, nitrates at the salad bar, or getting reprimanded as a kid. The truth is that all of this can play a role in our depression along with chemical imbalances and other health-related conditions. Depression comes from who-knows-where, but environment, genetics, diet, exercise, and stress all play a part in its makeup. No matter how many people share this malady, depression is a day-to-day struggle, you have to tend to yourself.

Lord, we flee to you for rescue from our enemies, both
inside and outside ourselves. Please save us.

11

Thoughts of Suicide

"I am utterly spent and crushed; I groan because of the
tumult of my heart" (Psalm 38:8).

I described the thought of suicide to a therapist one time as "having a full bladder and nowhere to go." It is the constant, urgent, conscious decision to hold it—or in the case of thoughts of suicide, to not follow through with your plan, even though the pressure is so severe and nearly to the point of exploding from loss of control. When you are emotionally, mentally, spiritually, or physically ill—when you are in so much pain your misery consumes every ounce of your being—thoughts of suicide can be very persuasive. Thinking that physical death will eliminate physical pain plus all the other illness is inviting, *but don't give in to suicide.*

Why? Because God approves of you just the way you are, and no matter the pain, God will hold it with you and for you. God will help; I know this to be true. Think of your family and friends. Your suicide literally destroy them. Maybe that is your goal—to destroy those around you by one selfish act. The problem with this is that you won't be around to know if any of it makes any difference. You may be an obituary one day, and that might be it, or you may be an obituary one day and hold many people hostage for years in the torment of what you have done—but you won't know this, because you won't be around to see it. Call someone. Talk to someone. Call 911. Get help. It is okay to get help; that's why help is there.

> *God of life, you feel our pain and know our torment. We*
> *trust you and know the most loving thing we can do is to*
> *live to love you another day. Sometimes, Lord, the pain is*
> *so severe and overwhelming, we see no way out; everything*
> *is black. Shine on us, O Lord. Bring us light.*

12

Getting Through Each Day

"Do not be grieved, for the joy of the Lord is your strength"
(Nehemiah 8:10b).

Depression wanders in the subjective world of gloom and doom. Words like *despair, fear, desperation, helplessness, hopelessness, death, uselessness,* and *worthlessness* become reality. These subjective words of depression have a way of manifesting themselves into objective reality. I realize that this particular objective reality is my perception. It may not be someone else's reality or perception, but that does not make my state of mind any less real. Try explaining black ooze on your ceiling to someone who doesn't see it. The very concept of an altered state of reality—though it makes perfect sense to me—does not settle with some people. The inability to define this altered sense of my world into a language understood by other people is sad.

I often have a sense of gloom and feel everything is dark, sad, and miserable. These subjective, non-tangible feelings of darkness, sadness, and misery spill over into the tangible world I am thrust into. This sense of gloom has no measurement of time. For example, 8:00 a.m. becomes 11:00 a.m. without my knowledge of time moving. It isn't a blackout; it is a complete disinterest in time and a total zoning out. Time doesn't matter in this place of gloom. Time makes no difference to my well-being; the nature of depression is that time holds no immediate need for me. Time is lost, because time is meaningless; all time is dark, sad, and miserable.

In an attempt to break this cycle, I fought hard to have an interest in time. On a day when I was feeling better, I set the TV to come on at 4:00 p.m. with *Judge Judy,* a half-hour show that stated facts. I had no processing to do other than to observe the show once it came on. The judge settles small claim suits people have against each other. That's it—nothing for me to process, decide, or figure out; it is a simple, matter-of-fact, half-hour show. At first, when the show clicked on at 4:00 p.m., I needed to make a difficult and conscious decision to listen. As a few days passed, I found I was listening *and* watching. In time, I found myself checking the clock to see how soon it was until 4:00 p.m. This simple process of behavior modification (though very difficult to do) helped me to break the cycle of gloom and doom.

The break from the gloom expanded until it included time after *Judge Judy* to watch *Jeopardy.* Now *Jeopardy* requires some concentration, brain power, and thought. Again, it took a while, but I found I was engaged with the show. Overall, this process of setting the clock to watch TV gave me permission to not be gloomy. It helped. In fact, I viewed it as a major success. It took great energy to do this, and it wasn't a cure-all, but it sure did help.

From this experience, I decided to break down each and every inability I had and attempt to engage in it. First was brushing my teeth. This should be on automatic pilot, but it took energy, thought, and motivation. There were many days I didn't have the energy to brush my teeth. This is odd, because I'm an avid brusher, even to the point of usually carrying a folding toothbrush in my purse. But when I am depressed, I am physically too tired and exhausted to brush. There was something else reducing my motivation, too, and it took some time to put it all together. Soon I realized that if I brushed my teeth, it was one small step to getting ready to leave the house, and there was no way I was leaving the house.

Fear was the deep feeling that was controlling my lack of brushing. So based on this discovery, I started setting a certain time in the evening to brush my teeth, because we wouldn't be going out of the house. As simple as it sounds, the whole process is taxing. My rule was that I would brush my teeth at night when I took my medicine. I even moved my toothbrush so I had to touch it to reach my pill dispenser as a reminder. As elementary and contrived as all this seems, it was a small way of gaining back some control. The only question I have is why on God's green earth someone didn't tell me about this method. It certainly can't be a brand new theory of treatment. The answer is quite simple; other than immediate family and health care providers, few people knew I was that sick.

To summarize this simple method: state the problem (how does this problem show up?), come up with some achievable goal, and take steps to reach the goal. You will need someone to help you remember—someone to whom you can be accountable who is motivational without being too cheerful!

The diagnoses of Major Depressive Disorder even has its own abbreviation—MDD. I didn't know how wonderful it would be to have an actual diagnosis. The symptoms range from mild to moderate cases to severe depression. That's me—severe depression. Statistics show relapses of major depressive episodes within two years of the last episode. That fits. My first major dive was in August of 2000. That episode had staying power, lasting well into February of 2001. Six months of being hunkered down in the corner of the couch is a long time. It was another year and a half before I was functioning well enough to maneuver through my days. It was an absolutely horrible time.

The next major episode started in September of 2003 and escalated for months—finally to the point of having to resign my job. Starting in January of 2005 and continuing for the next three years, I really struggled to gain control and confidence. Because of two major episodes, statistically I have an 80 percent chance of having another episode. So please be proactive with your own care, and use preventative measures as much as possible. It is really hard to use preventative measures after a major bout of depression, because it seems you are inevitably setting yourself up for another attack. However, maybe with good preventative care, you can abort another episode.

You will develop your own set of coping skills—some healthy and some not so healthy. Share your coping mechanisms with your therapist. Some of the coping skills I have used over the years have varied. Some have become rather obsessive and compulsive, such as cleaning, spending money, organizing things, peeling apples or potatoes (yes, it's strange), or drawing. The last skill I have acquired—drawing—has actually proven to be beneficial, because it has added to my income.

Each season holds its own set of wonders and setbacks. For me, winter is the time to really be diligent, because it is my most vulnerable time. Being proactive, establishing predetermined projects, and planning getaways is essential during this time. Be strong and learn about yourself. You are worth each and every effort taken toward leading a health-filled life.

> *God, your Son chose the path to pain before joy and the*
> *cross before glory so we don't have to. Thank you.*

Part 3

13

Blackbird Comes Calling

*"O that I had wings like a dove! I would fly away and be
at rest" (Psalm 55:6).*

I am a person who can and has taken on large and major activities
and projects, including all the details of planning, rehearsing,
organizing, and advertising. But sometimes it is difficult to make a
grocery list, let alone get to the store. Where is it that I go? When
do I go there? Oddly enough, a clue does come my way when a huge
episode of depression looms. Some call it an aura—a certain sense
of impending illness, a notion of things getting out of sequence, or
some clue in my gut.

The blackbird first showed up in August of 2000 as I was in
the tenth week of a ten-week clinical. A nasty experience with a
supervisor who thought making me bust into tears—or better said,
breaking me—was essential to my learning curve. The breaking
took place within the last two days before the end of the rotation. I
felt pretty good, having kept him at bay for the full ten weeks, and I
thought I may have bypassed the experience. My classmates had not
been so lucky, for over the course of ten weeks, he crumbled each
and every one of them.

There was quite a smile on his face when he realized he found a weak spot in my veneer. For a full five hours one day, he kept chiding me, pushing me, and forcing me to collapse—and I did. Once he had accomplished his dirty deed, his personal satisfaction was unbearable. He said to my classmates, "You won't see this too often." I'm not exactly sure what he meant by that except that I did know he felt a victory of some sort. This experience destroyed me. All the personal coping skills I had acquired over the years were gone.

The last two nights at this clinical site were torture. Black oily goo oozed from the ceiling of my room. It snuck out of the corners of the floorboards and hovered over my bed. With my Bible open to Isaiah, I read and read, but when I would doze off to sleep, I was startled awake again by this black ooze nearly sitting on my face. As soon as I started reading out loud again, the black ooze would move back toward the ceiling. If I stopped reading, it sunk down towards me yet again. It was horrifying. *So this is what becoming totally unglued is like,* I remember thinking to myself. I knew what was happening—I'm no idiot—but I had no clue what to do about it.

Each morning for ten weeks, I walked to the hospital, where the clinical was held on a beautiful road that wound through overhanging trees and old pines reaching up high. I looked forward to this walk, content and blessed as I strolled along, but on the first morning after fighting off the devil all night, I entered the winding road and was verbally attacked by blackbirds. A classmate came up just then, immediately felt my distress, and covered my head with his jacket. We ran for the building. This was a psychotic episode at its best.

The blackbird haunts me, forcing me to retreat, take shelter, or completely alter what I am doing or about to do. I do know when the blackbird shows up, my life goes to hell. Many times this damn bird has squelched my joy and hopes, forcing me to duck down and hide for fear of getting picked to death.

Being the proud person I am, there was no way I was going to let this supervisor know the damage he had caused to my psyche. Once again, the veneer appeared solid, the shell was intact, and there was no way he was getting in. Thus the beginning of the aura and the beginning of a thicker veneer.

Those damn birds have haunted me ever since. On the seminary campus that fall, those who knew my fear waited for me at the doors to walk with me to other buildings or dodge with me into a safe place. The picture window in my third-floor apartment which hung out over a fabulous cliff covered with trees, once a refuge, was now shut off, because the curtains were always drawn for fear of the blackbird. On the occasion I would open the drapes, blackbirds came by in droves to fill the trees, cawing unmercifully.

The blackbird comes calling on a bitter cold winter morning where the sun blinds my eyes. It is a world of static; there is no movement or life. All is frozen—dead, cold, and gone. Don't squawk at me, you stupid bird; don't remind me. How dare you, black devil, rip at my coat? Just fly on past; leave me alone. Have you no other place to be but to come by and bring reminders of being frozen, dead, cold, and gone? Blackbird, your caw is piercing and deadly, hanging in the trees. You are pitch black and staring with your black devil companions—copycats of you—all evil and cunning, so shameless, so putrid, swooping down on my head when I walk across green grass. You grip me with fear and peck out my guts, you evil bird. Get back. Get away. I spend no day without that devil blackbird of hate; even in summer, you enter my room with a vengeance, oozing down from the ceiling and out of the walls. You entered my soul with your sinister ways. Damn blackbird comes calling.

You may have an aura, too. Someone close to you may sense the coming of depression before you do. Listen to them. For me, the old birdie brings the dread, and when the old birdie has no effect on me, I know I am getting better. But back to the original question—where do I go when the blackbird comes calling? Like no other illness, depression threatens the "who: of you, and depression takes you to places unimaginable.

> *God of hope, your Word comes to me today in your*
> *promises to be faithful. Keep me close to your Word, and*
> *help me to always trust in your promise.*

14

Count Me In

"I have said this to you, so that in me you may have peace. In the world you face persecution. But take courage, I have conquered the world" (John 16:33).

By taking a good look at internal care, how to nurture the self, and the renewing of life—mind, body, and soul—I have found so many differences, I wasn't sure what to believe or turn to. Renewal is a continual process for our own health. We would give proper insulin to the diabetic, check out a raging fever on one of our children, avoid certain foods if we had Crohn's disease, or take medicines prescribed for our asthma; thus we must also take proper care of our depression. It is hard to wake up each morning and crank yourself up to get out of bed just to find you are walking through mud all day, exhausted, calculating your energy, and preoccupied. We talk freely about other conditions or maladies, but not depression—it still carries a stigma. It is a threat to others who fear the unknown. Even though we live in a society of epidemic conditions of overload and depression, it is easy to turn the other way. Depression is a feeling of being overwhelmed by the very need to breathe and stay alive, yet it is often discarded as being a person's own fault. At its worst, it is considered a malady of the unfaithful or those weak in belief of God.

Two well-known cases of depression would be Winston Churchill, who at the age of sixty-five became Prime Minister of England. He stayed in office through the late 1930s and '40s during WWII. Churchill survived on four to five hours of sleep at night, Bourbon, cigars, his wife Clementine, family, oil painting, the war room, and 20 Downing Street. He was plagued with depression. It isn't known how much of his depression was genetic, but from the life he led, it seems overwhelming feelings and an intense life were certainly contributing factors.

Another well-know man who experienced depression is Mike Wallace, the newscaster. From his penthouse in New York, he would look out over the city and cry, damning himself for giving in to the black shroud. As I have stated before, depression knows no boundaries; it can attack and destroys life wherever it can.

God of all life, helps us to live our lives for you and you alone.

15

The Church and the Depressed

It is difficult for us to admit our powerlessness. We spend
years building the illusion that we are in control only to face
events that make it clear that we have no control at all.

The greatest fear I have for the church is it lapsing into mere
doctrine, freeze-drying the gospel into a fixed formula—one stated
to be tried and true—and watering down the sense of location, state,
and condition of the present gospel reader. This courts danger, for
the continuing process of our injecting ourselves with some extra
dose of Christ from the outside does not allow us to cut the rope
and fall into the arms of Christ. For those of us who live with and
in depression, we meet Christ by entering into a space occupied
by Christ, entirely submerged in our own meeting place. In this
place lives the greatest perplexity of all, for only in this particular
space do we learn from the inside out about Christ helping us with
depression.

Some explanation is necessary to fit this together. In years of
attempting to be fixed, tended to, and soothed so as to be real, I
realized that all were processes from the outside. All the prayers
and longings for God and the despair and shuddering for the Holy
Spirit to hold me relieved pain immeasurably. But to find the

courage to enter deeply into the unknown—to open my eyes in the darkness and be unprotected and exposed to the abyss in order for Christ to catch me—seemed nearly impossible. I suppose this echoes of the theology of the cross, because the potential death of God on the cross is what we participate in unconditionally in the creation of our healing. It is because the cross did not win that I know I can enter the gap of depression and live. Major depression attacks the spirit, exploding a true feeling of abandonment even from God, which transpires into "many bleak moments," as Oscar Wilde described it.

Suffering is one very long moment. We cannot divide it by seasons. We can only record its moods and chronicle their return. With us, time itself does not progress; it revolves. It circles around one center of pain. For the depressed, there is only one season—the season of sorrow. The very sun and moon seem taken from us. Outside, the day may be blue and gold, but the light that creeps down through the thickly muffled glass of the small, iron-barred window beneath which one sits is gray and black. It is always twilight in one's cell, as it is always twilight in one's heart. And in the sphere of thought—no less than in the sphere of time—motion is no more.

The thing that you personally have long forgotten or can easily forget is happening now and will happen to me again tomorrow. Prosperity, pleasure, and success may be rough and tough, but sorrow is the most sensitive of all created things. There is nothing that stirs in the whole world of thought to which sorrow does not vibrate in terrible and exquisite pulsation. Where there is sorrow, there is holy ground. Some people will know nothing of life till they step foot on the holy ground of sorrow.

I will have to say my experience with the church has been quite disconcerting, and it is one I still am pioneering and pursing so others don't suffer alone needlessly at the hands of the church. Since the church is the body of Christ, there are flaws to this body. There are the occasional zits and warts, scrapes and bruises, but for those with depression, the church truly appears to be blind.

This is a strong statement, but I seriously have found very few pastors who accept and help people with depression—partly from their own feelings of inadequacy to the condition and in part due to an underlying notion it is not controllable anyway. One pastor I served alongside had a church member who was in and out of the psych ward repeatedly with depression and suicidal tendencies. Not once did he go to see her. In fact, she became a brunt of some jokes: "Got rid of her again." "She spends half her life up there to avoid doing anything." I have heard colleagues demean schizophrenia, bipolar disorder, dissociative identity disorder, and depression. The pastors with the compassion and empathy for mental illness and emotional struggles are truly gems and in many cases have experienced it firsthand in some capacity.

Finding a clergy person who understands depression, is willing and capable of discussing it openly and honestly, and most importantly, offers pastoral care for and during your depression is difficult. The only way I have gotten serious pastoral care was on my own prodding and pushing. It most definitely didn't come to me or my family without very strong and specific demands upon clergy.

During my lowest points, God provided one particularly awesome colleague and confidant (thanks, ML). Other than this person, my own denomination had nothing to do with me except to offer superficial advice and wash its hands of me.

As the divine pathos pushes and presses to participate with creation, I do believe God will unconditionally stay with me to the end until I am healed and beyond. I know this because in baptism, I was baptized into this death. In baptism, my life became directed toward the world where Christ's life is, and Christ is with the excluded ones. Depression puts us in an excluded category—oddly enough, particularly in the church—for this malady takes our spirit, but Christ fills our souls. All this suffering allows me to have a brush with God's astonishing compassion. Since there is pain in the world and God became human by choice, God is willing to suffer. This is the highest identity to have with another—to suffer with him or her. Christ is utterly gracious to feel this hurt with me.

God knows suffering from the inside out. This divine, astonishing compassion for this human wretch who lives at best in frail uncertainty frees me to live. We go to great lengths to fend off questions and discourage thought so we don't have to face our own ignorance and uncertainties, but we ignore Christ. As we permit doubt to be vital in our life, the grace of faith leads us to a true belief and unswerving trust that the quest may continue without fear of losing our way.

Inner theological debate keeps Christ active in this process of muddled-ness. At times, the whole notion of God seems made up to pacify a sick mind. But I have dismissed the absence of God; God is here. Do I push on into greater despair to see if Jesus really will be there with me? Does knowing Christ come with such cost? I look with confidence for God's grace in this reality of depression.

In all the frantic moments—the delusions and hallucinations, panic and apnea—just as hopelessness conquers, relief (however minute) comes. A new thought, an incoming prayer, some other diversion, such as a cat jumping on my lap—whatever God sends, it is lavished upon me. This is the key to it all. In the lavished love of God, I have the confident expectation that a desire for relief will be fulfilled perfectly.

The quest for understanding and the commitment to thought is never satisfied. My greatest human endeavor is to understand the reason for this need to have such a wart as depression. If God truly wants to know me, must this honest relationship be through suffering? No beginning or end is seen; all I know is this blessedness and condition of oneness with Christ, day in and day out. The sphere within is deemed reality, because here hard-fought freedom has been granted.

Gracious God, your church is difficult to understand and
to live in. However, we also understand the necessity of the
church for the lives of the faithful and the mission
of your saving grace.

16

Inside the Depressed Mind

"You will have pain, but your pain will turn into joy"
(John 16:20b).

Chronology or straight lines do not share the story, for depression is not linear. Depression revolves around some unidentified force. The force of gravity can help describe this pull on me, and I must use all my strength to pull away from depression; it is strong and unrelenting. Once I am pulled in—once I am pulled completely off balance—I enter a different arena. This is a hollow place void of everything and anything. There is nothing here—nothing at all—just a purple-black hollow, a large gap. The presence of this gap fades in and out of my direct thinking, but it is always there while nothing else is.

The word *gap* totally describes this place of hollowness for me. When I'm depressed, this gap—this empty space—is impermeable, limitless, and has no boundary or ending. I fight to get out, and the only way out is the way I came in. There is only one speck of light.

The total awareness of essential good and inevitable evil meet here. Christ is always the victor, but a battle always ensues, taking place here, and it seems to be my very soul that is fought over. At the same time the battle takes place, the gap appears to be the only network in my brain, and it takes every ounce of non-thinking to allow this battle to take place. I know full well that Christ will come out victorious. This phenomena evidentially brings me to Christ. Even in the worst of all battles, I can be still and know that God is present. However, I have also wondered if this is only an illusion of rest, thus enticing me into the gap when all along, it is chaos that will have its way.

When people with depression seem to disappear—when there is no expression, spontaneity, or recognition of life-living—it is because the insides go numb. The insides become a battle ground so noisy and scary that complete retreat is the only safe place. There have been times I think I am having a mental experience of perceiving what takes place in the gap, but the thoughts are not my own, because I have been rendered incapable. Though this hollow—this gap—is completely void, the battle ensues here.

At other times, there appear to be elements in this hollow space—elements such as atoms of different sizes. When I'm pulled into this gap, I too become an element, and I become exhausted in my attempt to avoid plowing into another element. Einstein fluidly spoke of "togetherness in separation" in his general relativity theory. It fits for depression too. All elements within the gap move to a separate pulse and have a separate entity. Each is different; each responds to the pull of the perceived center based on past experience. I too am one of these elements—or so it seems. What I have discovered is that I totally wear myself out by avoiding the other elements, which all appear more powerful than me. As I exhaust myself trying to avoid the other entities in this hollow space, the central pull is always to a center where chaos rules. It is exhausting to not give in to depression! No matter how it is phrased or worded, the matter of pulling away, avoiding entering, and battling—if pulled in—is absolutely exhausting.

I discovered if I gave in to this pull and totally relinquished my struggle—though it is a black beacon of destruction I see—I really fall into the arms of Jesus. In the arms of Jesus, I am no longer separate but safe. It is in this determined togetherness where grace lives. This is freedom of choice—this is free will—either exhausting myself to stay separate from the depression or surrendering all to the pulse of Jesus.

Mind you, the pulse of Jesus also works in and through the many wonderful health care and mental health care providers available. Jesus is not a substitute for intelligent medical care; Jesus is the reason there is intelligent medical care.

As simple as these psychotic meanderings within this gap appear at first, it is exquisitely sensitive to all circumstances. The slightest disturbance and every element behave or fall into a very different pattern; thus for me, being still (nearly catatonic) on the sofa enables the necessary calm. As each element changes its positioning, I too must change and divert my course, or I will get struck by yet another element. Being stuck by an element within the hollow represents the simple forces of the outside world—at least, that's how I've come to witness it—for the whole of this life becomes intrinsically unpredictable. As you think about moving through a regular day at work, the depressed person also needs to have a regular day in the life of depression. Too much interference or change results in some form of chaos.

Consciousness begins in the gap—the hollow—in a time between morning and night, a time between dawn and dusk in which one is never fully awake or fully asleep. I'm not sure when this place became known to me—it has been there for years, but no beginning comes to mind. It possibly came with the emergence of my own consciousness, though the chasm existed before I did. More curious to me is when this space became aware of itself. When did this battleground between good and evil know it was the source of my energy?

There was a time I fought off this place. In all likelihood, my reluctance to enter this hollow was a sign of my reluctance to enter the real world. Christ insists on our entering the real word. Christ insists we encounter the real world. Maintaining our own exclusion by working so hard to remain separate severely limits faith. By faith, our goal to include the other actually translates into the need to be included. Only faith insists on being the included one and meets up with Christ by falling into his arms.

I realize all these wonderings appear to be the musing of a disturbed mind. This could be, though it is for this very reason these musings need to be shared. The completely erroneous groupings of "us—those who are excluded because of depression—provides yet another way for us to become included into yet another dimension of Jesus' participation in our lives.

"And immediately they left their nets and followed him"
(Mark 1:18).

17

Anxiety

"And no kind of harm was found on him, because he had trusted in his God" (Daniel 6:23a).

Anxiety may start as worry about something unpleasant that may have happened or may happen. Anxiety is a troubled, unsettling feeling which happens in the present time. Anxiety can get hold of you and take you on a horrific tailspin of fear, concern, unease, and dread. You sense your pulse racing and your breathing becoming sporadic, and you know something must change to eliminate this imposing sensation of total loss of control. Anxiety can start slowly, moving into your being through time, or it may nail you when you least expect it. Panic may squeeze your chest like there is no tomorrow.

For me, the most disturbing part of anxiety is the personal loss of control. It becomes a battle between inner calm and inner chaos. It disrupts peace, centeredness, and the feeling of self-trust. It is vitally important to get a hold of anxiety before it gets a hold of you, so do follow through on appropriate preventative measures and discuss them with your doctor. Your doctor may prescribe some anti-anxiety medication. It is okay to take it. Anxiety has the ability to affect personal honor, self-esteem, self-confidence, and self-respect. Be good to yourself. Take care of yourself. Abide in the Lord. *"I can do nothing on my own"* (John 5:30).

When anxiety settles in, try to do something objective in your mind, or say it out loud if you need to. The multiplication tables help me—especially the harder ones that make me think, such as 13x6=78, 13x7=91, 13x8=104, or 17x3=51. Recite the major chords with the flats or sharps. Name the colors on the color chart and what color appears when you mix other colors. As you think through something very concrete that has an answer, it may lessen the immediate anxiousness.

If your anxiety is persistent or if the heart palpations continue, see your doctor to rule out other maladies, such as a cardiac arrest. Emergency rooms see people periodically who present with cardiac symptoms but are suffering panic attacks. Believe me; a panic attack is no less threatening than a heart attack to the person suffering with it.

Prevention is key. If possible, avoid anxiety-producing situations. Not all situations can be avoided, such as going to the dentist, but take the time before your dental appointment to talk to the dentist about your concerns and what measures can be taken before and during your appointment to relieve anxiety. Some situations can be avoided, such as going to big, bright stores or avoiding small spaces. If it is possible, avoid situations that increase anxiety. Anxiety is often framed around worry—worry about something that has happened or worry may happen. There are many recommended measures you can try to eliminate chronic worry and generalized anxiety. Here are a few ideas that work for me:

- Deep breathing—stop what you are doing, and take a very deep breath in through your nose. Hold it for as long as you can, and then blow it out through your mouth. Then consciously think about your breathing, and envision the air going in through your nose and out through your mouth. This will offer some immediate relief.

- Try a "palms up, palms down" prayer. Begin by placing your palms down to symbolize your desire to turn concerns over to God. Turn whatever is bothering you or weighing you down over to God. Then turn your palms up to receive God's calming effect.

- Focus on a piece of art, burn a scented candle, get fresh flowers, play music, or get a massage. It is good to honor yourself and care for yourself. Be still before God. God wants to spend time with you. God is telling you, "I'll take care of the hard stuff, and I will take care of you." "Be still and know that I am God" (Psalm 46:10).

- Try to empty out your mind. This is particularly difficult but worth the effort. Be in a safe place where you can close your eyes and be comfortable. Listen to all the different sounds and noises around you, and identify them—the furnace running, the faucet dripping, a car driving by—just listen for a while. Then one by one, slowly block the noise out of your mind. I start with the least obvious, like the car driving by; only listen then to the dripping and the furnace. Then eliminate the dripping from your mind. Finally, attempt to not hear the furnace.

- I refer to yesterday's crayons, because for me, coloring is very calming. I can sit, zone out, and calm down while coloring. I have a sketchbook and many colored markers. Do old-fashioned scribble art where you close your eyes and scribble around on the page and then open your eyes to your creation. The fun part is filling in the spaces.

◆ Listen with your heart. John 17:6-19 is called the high priestly prayer of Jesus, and it is very important to listen to, because in this prayer, the demands Jesus makes of God are for us. The requests in this prayer are imperative to our lives. Jesus is soon to meet his death, yet he prays for us with fervor, passion, and strength, his arms lifted up to God. I encourage you to read the whole text, for in it, Jesus refers to us more than thirty times. He puts us front and center and demands from God that we be protected, guarded, and sanctified. You can feel the desire Jesus has for your eternal welfare and your eternal safety.

18

Abide with Me

I received the living God, and my heart is full of joy.

Jesus tells us, "Abide in me and I in you" (John 6:51-58). There is a
song about abiding that comes to mind: "Abide with me, fast falls
the eventide / the darkness deepens, Lord, with me abide." *(Henry
F. Lyte) Abide* means "to bear patiently," "constant," and "enduring."
We want Christ to abide in us and bear us up patiently—to be
constant and understanding. We want Christ to be enduring,
everlasting, and never to give up on us. But not only does Jesus say,
"Abide in me," but he also says, "and I in you." Thus we are to bear
patiently, being constant in our faith and understanding of Christ
abiding in us. Christ abides in us. Christ lives in us. Christ inhabits
our very beings.

Every morning brings a new struggle to push through. You do
not have your belief once and for all. Either we receive faith anew
every day or it deteriorates. "None of us is so rushed that it would
be impossible to allow for even ten minutes in the day in which
arrangements could be made for silence, in order to place oneself in
the presence of Eternity" (Dietrich Bonhoeffer). Anxiety can be one

of the most frightening, overwhelming experiences in the world. Take care to take care.

You have put on Christ; in him you have been baptized.

Part 4

19

Rejoice

Rejoice, the Lord is king.

It's party day—the first day of the rest of your life? It is the beginning of an all-new era of existing and a great day. The theme of the day is *rejoicing*.

Is anyone missing? Are there missing family members or friends to rejoice with you? Who did you expect would be here? Are you missing the enthusiasm to have a great day? Are you missing the passion to have a good day? Maybe you are just trying to get through the day.

Yet it is the first day. Despite all the gloom and doom, it is a day to invite someone—anyone—a friend, neighbor, or family member back in to your life. Today you will rejoice. Today you will undertake the reality that life is worth rejoicing and worth rejoicing with another.

The importance of our rejoicing and figuratively celebrating is being sure we bring to us those who are absent. The list of the missing must be looked at closely with arrangements made to contact each and every one, because if one is missing, we are not complete, and the party is not the same, such as a family reunion.

There is much to do and think about before a party. Yet despite all the effort—all the thought and planning that goes into a celebration of rejoicing—you must find it necessary to invite someone to rejoice with you. We must be sure to connect with our missing and remember them as we pray for their connection with us which fills the holes in our hearts. When all are present or our relationship with them is determined once for all, then all our senses can rejoice. It takes work to prepare for a party; it takes work to celebrate relationships and to rejoice. Today is a day to rejoice. Rejoice with me.

> *Thank you, God, for my many friends and family*
> *members; however, I push them away. Please help me to*
> *reconnect with even one of my loved ones today.*

20

Don't Go It Alone

God is love. God is light. God is everlasting!

A few years ago, twin hippopotami were born in the Memphis zoo. A contest to name the hippo twins ensued. The only hitch was that the mother hippo wouldn't let anyone close enough to the babies to determine their sex. Apparently the two forty-pound babies walked just under their mother, and no one wanted to upset a momma who weighs more than a luxury limo by getting too close. I don't know exactly what a hippo does to protect her young, but I suspect it isn't pleasant. The mother continued to care for her babies by feeding them, protecting them, and keeping them close to herself and away from danger. And the babies, untroubled by their nameless state, didn't stray from their mother. Why should they stray? As young and naïve as they were, they still knew a good thing when they saw it. The babies stayed close to their momma—close to food, protection, warmth, and nurturing.

You won't find kittens turning away from the warm fur they know so well in their mother. Chicks don't stray far from the protection of the hen's wings. Most assuredly, this is instinct, and the least intelligent animal offspring stay close to the one who gave them life. But people—well, that's another story. Humans stray, and the children of God turn away from the love and protection of the God who made them.

Depression ravages the mind, body, and soul; it becomes so encompassing that turning to God for protection becomes too difficult. What then? God hears the sounds of the breaking heart with the fierce love of a mother and has not left you alone. When we agonize over something in our lives or if depression refuses to allow relationships with others, God is there even when we may feel very alone. We need to collapse under the holy wings, for there is comfort. Often depression turns life in a series of staccato notes, and we find ourselves pecking here and there in the hopes that we may stumble upon some morsel that will nub our minds and take our thoughts away. And during this time, you may not even realize you have wandered from the protection of God.

Depression feeds off the vastness of the day's troubles: the irritations, hassles, and problems of work, school, or family. We come home and anesthetize our minds with food and drink, household chores and hobbies, TV, family problems, family joys, even church commitments—any and everything to keep from looking depression in the face. But this busyness to ward off depression can distance us and put a strange silence from God in our lives. God always beckons and calls us to huddle under the outstretched wings, warm and secure next to the beating heart of God. Even now, God bids us to come, trust, and rely on God's protection, nurturing, and guidance through our harrowing days.

Where animals can and will protect and care for their young for a time, God pledges love and nurturing for an eternity. This is true security—true protection whatever pain or problems may plague us, fear may face us, or sin may assail us. We will never be found defenseless or alone. We stand under the protection of God's wings, shaded by God's forgiveness, strengthened by the body and blood which come to us.

A story goes about the day a hen house burned down. The farmer arrived just in time to help put out the last of the fire. As the wreckage was being sorted through, he came upon one hen lying dead near what had been the door of the hen house. Her top feathers were browned by the fire's heat; her neck was limp. He bent down to pick up the dead hen, and four chicks came scurrying out from beneath her burnt body. The chicks survived, because they were insulated by the shelter of the hen's wings, protected and saved even as she died to protect and save them. Christ affords each one of us such protection from the fires of life. Christ's life was taken as you were saved and protected from the devastating impact of depression. You can trust him no matter what fears, hurts, or troubles tug you to go it alone. Stay put under the protection and care of Jesus Christ.

"I wait for the Lord, my whole being waits, in him I put
my hope." (Psalm 130:5).

21

Take A Hike

*"Trust in the Lord with all your heart, and do not rely on
you own insight" (Proverbs 3:5).*

During one overwhelming time at seminary, I was talking to one of
the professors, and he sensed my intense feeling of being so bogged
down that I didn't know what to do first. His advice: take a walk.
Taking a walk wasn't a thinking proposition. As I strolled around,
I looked at the neighborhood flowers and yards. I walked along
the boulevard, admiring the fabulous flower beds designed by the
city, and I noticed the golf course. I headed into the course, just
observing, watching the gofers tee off—some with smoothness
and skill, some ax-chopping the ball, and others with a very rigid
mechanical swing—and through all this, I was diverted from being
overwhelmed.

There are many things you can do—listen to music, walk, do
something you view as one of your strengths, play piano, grill a pork
chop, or play catch. Do something you are good at which affirms you.

But like so many things, all this is a diversion. As great as these
getaways can be, for me they are still a momentary fix. So I set
out to find something which gives me a permanent connection for
dealing with overwhelmed feelings.

Walking and meditating, fishing, or gardening are all ways to help us feel less overwhelmed, but I wanted to rely on something more specific and particular.

Some true statements which I preach and teach are:

"Let go and let God," "Turn it over to the Lord," "You are never alone; Christ is always with you," and "The Holy Spirit will hold you up." We take these statements as truth, knowing other, short-term remedies are just that—short-term. These remedies include "Let go and let golf," "Turn it over to the hot tub," "You are never alone; you have your traveling labyrinth," or "The gardening will hold you up." As great as these things are, I need to live in total surrender. The quick fix was not enough; I wanted and needed more.

The feeling of being overwhelmed is not to be taken lightly. It often accompanies depression and/or anxiety. It can be very intense and make you feel under attack. The feeling is an attack on who you are, for your psyche cannot realistically put you in all the places and positions you need to be, and the feeling is overwhelming. The "who" of you is attacked, and you may momentarily psychologically leave for a while, losing your identity as you search for resolution to the feeling of being overwhelmed.

We don't know how to say we are "intensed" out. Generally we feel inadequate in the situation. We may feel irresponsible, insufficient, negligent, or stupid. It is necessary to work on what to do with your overwhelmed feelings, finding ways to look at, observe, disengage from, and learn from them.

Divide the reasons for being overwhelmed and the feelings accompanying them into smaller piece so you can look at the whole mess objectively and move away from the subjectivity having its way with you. We all have intensity about us. We all have moments of being overwhelmed when we feel we are in over our heads. Others may feel a fairly good balance, with an occasional bomb falling or an infrequent land mine being stepped on.

If you ever find yourself working harder to get the same amount done or fighting exhaustion just to find the next day to be worse, take a break. Truly momentary walks, exercise, mediation, and hot tub soaks may provide just the momentary fix we need to deal with the rest of it. As helpful as it can be and as necessary as they are, these fixes are still momentary. So what to do?

Something we often bypass personally and lump into the Sunday morning corporate confession is personal confession. Confession and absolution are the surrender of our personal will to the divine will. The power of the will—the higher will of God—moves us to a greater consciousness of what is really important. I find that the capacity to make decisions and the center of all my faith and knowledge comes through and with confession and absolution. This allows me to sort out what is necessary to attend to in overwhelmed times. It gives me my creative edge; permits inspiration to come to me unhindered; and opens up personal expression, discovery, and visioning. All these things move me into what I was created to be rather than sitting in a pile of overwhelmed feelings.

The power of our will up against the will of God is an interesting concept. The best thing you can do for yourself when you sense life's details engulfing you is run to your confessor and get your "umpf" back. Nothing provides cleansing, a new start, and healing like being absolved of your sins.

Oh God, help us to live Revelation 14:4:
"these follow the Lamb wherever he goes."

22

Where Is God in All this Depression?

"The Lord has heard my supplication; the Lord accepts my prayer" (Psalm 6:9).

Where is God in all this depression? Right beside you, holding you close. Does God make things happen? Yes, there is action in God, and we receive what a loving, caring God gives us. Having faith is the action of God, and we receive God. Religion is an attempt to gain something from God, so we "do" creeds, actions, and proper conduct in an attempt to gain God. But we don't need to do these things, because with simple faith, God walks, sits, and mourns with us. Where is God in all this depression? God is right beside you. God says, "I am your shield. Do not be afraid." It is God's good pleasure to give you the kingdom.

God, there are times you seem far away, but I know you are carrying me.

23

Faith

Lord, help my unbelief.

Faith is the assurance of things hoped for—the conviction of things not seen. By faith, we understand that God creates and that God is faithful to God's creation. We with depression live in a land of promise. God has fashioned your very heart. Faith is the lack of fear or fearing not, knowing God will care and provide for you. Do not worry; God will provide.

24

Healing

"O Lord, my God, I cried to you for help, and you have healed me" (Psalm 30:2).

"While he was saying these thing to them, suddenly a leader of the synagogue came in and knelt before him saying, 'My daughter has just died; but come and lay your hand on her, and she will live.' And Jesus got up and followed him, with his disciples. Then suddenly a woman who had been suffering from hemorrhages for twelve years came up behind him and touched the fringe of his cloak, for she said to herself. 'If I only touch his cloak, I will be made well.' Jesus turned and seeing her he said, 'Take heart, daughter; your faith has made you well.' And instantly the woman was made well. When Jesus came to the leader's house and saw the commotion, he said. 'Go away; for the girl is not dead but sleeping.' And they laughed at him. But when the crowd had been put outside, he went in and took her by the hand, and the girl got up and the report of this spread throughout that district." (Matthew 9:18-26). Matthew's gospel is very clear on the healing grace of Jesus. Out of nowhere, suddenly the father of the girl and the suffering woman are by Jesus, and instantly Jesus responds. Are you any less important than these? There is no doubt about the perpetuation of healing; Jesus heals.

The forever-ness of the healing is in the forever-ness of Jesus. In Jesus' perfect timing, we are healed instantly. Oh Christ, heal me in your perfect timing.

Part 5

25

Make a List and Check it Twice

*"But as for me, I know that my Redeemer lives, and that
he will stand upon the earth at last. And after my body
has decayed, yet in my body I will see God! I will see God
for myself. Yes I will see God with my own eyes. I am
overwhelmed at the thought!" (Job 19:25-27)*

Make a list of the people you can turn to for an intimate relationship.
By intimate, I mean personal, confidential, private, comfortable,
and in-depth. Take some time to fill in the following list with names
of people who currently fill these roles for you. If no one does, you
must view this list as a necessary project to complete. You should
have and need the following people in your life. Like most people,
you may not have anyone who comes to mind for any of these
important positions in your life. Now is as good a time as ever to
start considering who could fill these relationships for you. I read
or heard somewhere that children need at least seven adults in their
lives to have a strong, healthy upbringing. It seems to me adults
need that, too.

◆ 1. Who is your personal confessor, the person you can go to
and confess your sins?

- 2. Who feeds you the Word, reminding you of God's promises?
- 3. Who do you know who honors you through daily prayer?
- 4. Who do you go to for clarity of your thoughts?
- 5. Who do you talk to when you need a safe, private, confidential talk?
- 6. Who do you allow yourself to cry with?
- 7. Who believes for you when you cannot believe for yourself?
- 8. With whom can you divulge the things you're not proud of—your major mess-ups and most embarrassing moments?
- 9. Who reads the Bible to you?
- 10. Who tells you that you are a good person?

*Good and gracious God, you have blessed us with
numerous people of integrity in our lives. Help us to tap
into their potential and give them the opportunity to serve
you. Also, Lord, help us to fulfill these roles for others.*

26

Devotion

"What sort of man is this, that even the winds and the sea
obey him?" (Matthew 8:27b)

If possible spend (or try to spend) a part of your day or even a few minutes a day in devotion. When we are down, it is hard to have devotional time, because it takes energy just like everything else takes energy. Devotion can take on as many and varied forms, shapes, and visions as you need to express your love, repentance, intercessions, and praise to God. Through the days and years of depression, some of the devotionals I use are abbreviated here for you.

You can meditate in the spur of the moment. You can meditate with planning and forethought by adding fresh flowers, quiet music, hot tea, incense, water fountains, candles, pictures, icons, or a cross to your meditation space. Bring something to your surroundings which offers a simple stimulation to one or more of the senses—smell, sight, touch, taste, or sound.

Once you are in a place or in a space in time, prepare your heart by quieting the rumble inside. Your heart may be as depressed as you are with only emptiness there. That's okay. Call depression what it is, and move to a new space. Devote only as you have the ability to, for devotion is exercise for the soul and takes effort and determination.

If you must choose where to spend your energy, devotion to God should be at the top of the list, for without renewing, your emotional and spiritual life will stagnate.

An easy way I engage in meditation or devotion is through the acronym TRIP: thanksgiving, repentance, intercessions, and praise. All of these TRIP segments can be done in any number of ways or one at a time throughout the day or week. There is no right or wrong way to have devotions or to meditate.

Thanksgiving and praise come easy with lyrics to songs or hymns; say, repeat, or sing them. **R**epenting and asking God for forgiveness helps reach the soul and comfort the spirit. If indeed you do have someone to take your sins to, absolution with the laying on of hands is extremely meaningful. Make **i**ntercessions for yourself and others. **P**raise through lyrics or poems, praying, reading Scripture, reciting the Psalms, or invoking the Holy Spirit. Be still and calm, reflect, read devotions or personal stories, lay down your burdens with singing or chanting; these all are forms of devotion. Ponder, consider, be in the now, commemorate people who you hold close who have died—saints, family members, martyrs, mystics—study words or phrases, and move your mind. If you can move your body too, walk a labyrinth. Most of all, pray.

Dear God, we love you and cherish you. Help us to show
how much we need you. Lord, help us to pray as we ought
and to keep our focus on you.

27

You Have Not Fallen from Grace

"What are human beings, that you make so much of them,
that you set your mind on them, visit them every morning"
(Job 7:17).

You have not fallen from grace by having depression. Mental health challenges are real. Living with mental health concerns adds a dimension to your life others do not have. Remember that Jesus crosses the line with you. Jesus is in and within you during the paranoia, fear, and constant blues. You cannot will depression to be gone. You can relax in the arms of the Holy Spirit and be safe from harm. You are not fallen from grace but living in the midst of it. Imagine yourself in the middle of the triune God, being protected and cared for; there is nothing to fear. Relax, muster a smile, and be with the God of love and concern. You can do this.

Oh Christ of grace and mercy, here we are—safe in your care!

28

Hopelessness

"What are human beings, that you make so much of them,
that you set your mind on them, visit them every morning"
(Job 7:17).

She was fifteen years old and by all appearances was living life to its fullest. She was playing volleyball at school and had a very nice boyfriend who had his dad drive him over to her place to study or go swimming. She loved math and was in advanced algebra classes. By all appearances, she was young and full of life with a bright future ahead of her. Although this was the appearance to many, inside this girl, a war was going on. School was no longer satisfying, she didn't feel she deserved such a nice boyfriend, and the confident exterior gave way to an internal battle. She felt hopeless.

Why should she go on? There was nothing in this life for her. One day she had enough; she could no longer bear the emptiness she felt on the inside, and she ran away. She ran from home, her family, her school, and her friends.

Have you ever felt like a complete failure? Do you ever wonder what you are alive for? Has life seemingly passed you by? Do you lie awake at night and wonder why your life has turned out the way it has? Maybe at one point in your life you had big dreams and you were going places, but now you wonder why you live—why fight this battle anymore? Nothing really matters. It all adds up to hopelessness.

In our world today, many people feel like their existence means nothing. Many are simply empty shells of brokenness. They may paste smiles on their faces and laugh their way through life or become depressed and withdrawn from it all. There is the searching and longing cry of people living broken live and in fact, it is a world crisis. Where is the hope? Where is the peace? Where is the purpose and meaning of life here in this real world?

You may feel like you have messed up too many times and your time is up—that God would never forgive you now. You may think, "I've gone too far" or "I've waited too long." Perhaps the river of life has dried up. Have you ever wondered where your water supply for life is?

God desires to recast your broken vessel of life and to fill you with life. It doesn't matter how dried up your life may be, and it doesn't matter how shattered or broken it has become, for there is hope. God plans to make you all that God has intended you to be, and God wants to free you from your suffering, pain, and hopelessness. It doesn't matter what you have done or where you have been; God wants to fill you up. God has provided the redemption plan for your life through Jesus' conquering death and living again. In your despair, you say, "Who can save me?" Whisper the name of Jesus. Your life might be in shambles and all your hope gone, but God doesn't throw anyone away. There is hope.

The world around the fifteen-year-old girl dimmed for what she thought was the last time, but months later, she wondered if she had done the right thing by running away. She thought her life was dead, but God redeemed, remade, and refilled her vessel. If it had not been for God's mercy, she would not have lived. It is only through God and God's mercy that some of you are reading this today. We don't know the number of times God protects us. We don't know the number of times God has spared us. You may feel broken, but God has redeemed you.

Did you know there are a few things God cannot do?

◆ God cannot leave you.
◆ God cannot forsake you.
◆ God cannot stop loving you.
◆ God cannot forget you.
◆ God cannot neglect you.
◆ God cannot make a mistake.
◆ God cannot lose.
◆ God cannot be unforgiving to those who ask for forgiveness.
◆ God cannot stop thinking about you.

God, there are times our "calamity laid in the balances . . .
would be heavier than the sand of the sea" (Job 6:3).

29

Water as a Metaphor

*"Oh gives thanks to the Lord for he is good and his love
endures forever." (Psalm 118:1)*

What is depression without metaphors? Nearly every professional
person I have talked to or with over the last several years has come
to the same metaphor—water—and it is one of my own humors
within this whole time of searching for relief. Maybe this metaphor
is taught in counseling classes because it is prevalent. It's not that
it doesn't work; it just gets humorous over time. On my water
metaphor list are words or phrases I have heard: *sink or swim, sinking,
buoy, down for the count, treading water, rough waters, in a canoe
all alone, get pulled into a canoe, over the waterfall, flows, leaks, fills,
spills, wet, freezes, drown, splashing, emerged, mighty waters, stormy
seas, hurricanes,* and *dry creek bed.* The one word that brings me
marvelous pause is *baptism.*

I think the water metaphor is used because it is so natural and
universal. Water or the lack of water is something everyone can
relate to in some way. Water is actually a good metaphor and can be
helpful. Sometimes the metaphor is too narrow for how awful I'm
feeling, such as running a rapids is a different feeling than being in

a hurricane. Whatever the reason water is used so much, I do find it humorous at times.

The word baptism within the water metaphor brings me back to my roots, my child of God status, and my salvation. I have found depression to be evil at times. Baptism is the tarp protecting me from the storm.

Dear God, thank you for times of lightness and joviality
during these stormy patches. Thank you, God, for baptism
into the eternal life of Jesus Christ.

Part 6

30

The Ten Lepers

"Oh God You are my God" (Psalm 63:1).

"As he entered a village, ten lepers approached him. Keeping their distance, they called out, saying, 'Jesus, Master, have mercy on us!' When he saw them, he said to them, 'Go and show yourselves to the priests.' And as they went, they were made clean. Then one of them, when he saw that he was healed, turned back, praising God with a loud voice, He prostrated himself at Jesus' feet and thanked him . . . . Then Jesus said to him, 'Get up and go on your way; your faith has made you well'" (Luke 17:11-19).

This parable is of the ten lepers who stay some distance from Jesus and ask him to cleanse them from their disease. All they were looking for was someone to cure their illness—to clean their wounds and heal their sores. From what they had heard, Jesus was the one to perform this miracle. The ten lepers came to be healed, wanting to walk away whole and complete, without blemish and without problems. They cried, out "Jesus, Master, have mercy on us!"

Of course Jesus was compassionate and sent them to the priests. Then we are told they were cleansed as they went on their way before getting to the priests. We know one returned to Jesus, but all we know about the other nine is that they didn't come back to Jesus. No matter what the other nine did—run off, go to the temple, or stand in the courtyard praising their good fortune—they missed the point of being healed from leprosy. Only one returned to Jesus and fell on his face in front of Jesus to thank him for cleansing his leprosy.

By returning to Jesus, the cured leper was the only one healed of leprosy that day who was also *saved*. The flesh was healed for all ten, but the soul was saved for the one who realized it was Jesus who did the healing and the saving. One understood the real truth. The flesh was healed, but the one called Jesus is the one true God. The connection between God's miracle and Jesus is understood only by the one who returned. Jesus is more than a good guy with special gifts; Jesus is God.

What about us? Do we get it? Do we go to church to thank God but neglect to let Jesus save us? When is the last time you fell on your face at the feet of Jesus? We all have "fall on your face" moments. You know the moments and remember them—the moment you found out your baby girl was in critical care, the day all the crops were flooded out, the moment your spouse died, when cancer was announced, or when Parkinson's was the diagnoses. You know the moment when your face hits your hands and you turn all your burdens over to Jesus and thank him for taking them away. You thank him for loving you, giving you life, and giving you peace during times of despair.

The nine who ran off—healed as they were—may have gone to the temple. And we who run from the news of gloom or disaster may have run off to church. But do we fall on our face at the feet of Jesus at the moment. The moment the cancer is cured, the day the surgery fixes the baby's heart, the day the medicine gives relief to the Parkinson's, the day of resurrection after the death of your spouse—do you again fall on your face at the feet of Jesus, thanking the Lord for the blessed mercy? Jesus is right where we are; we don't have to wait to go to the church. We have no need to wait till Sunday.

We have a God in Jesus Christ and celebrated by the Holy Spirit—the living, ever-present God. And Jesus says to us—just as he proclaimed to the healed one—"Arise; go your way. Your faith has made you well."

God of love, thank you for being there for us when our
blemishes are more than we can bear.

31

The Promised Land

Moses was on the verge of suicide, and he hated his job. He was overwhelmed by the expectations of upper management. Executive responses to the demands of the people at the lowest levels had failed to satisfy. Frustrated with his supervisor and furious with his constituents, Moses was way past the point of turning in a resignation. When he lay in his bed roll at night, he just wanted to close his eyes and never open them again.

The people were not satisfied with manna; they wanted meat. They walked around mumbling, remembering the good old days back in Egypt when they had as much fish as they could eat—free of charge—with melons, onions, and cucumbers on the side for a small fee. Ah, the good old days. I have heard it said that the good old days are the product of a bad old memory. The people had forgotten that the same hands that fed them fish also cracked a whip across their back. They had forgotten that the ones who ran the farmer's market where they bought their onions and garlic were the same ones who forced them into harsh labor—a labor that made them too tired to have children, die from exhaustion in the desert heat, and perish at an early age. So we learn from the Hebrew children wandering in the wilderness that *a painful past is less frightening than an uncertain future.*

Life is like quicksand, where hope is faint and fading away, misery thrives, there is no vision for better things, and you are pulled down. Pulled down and dissatisfied, discontent, disappointed, despairing and depressed. It is like quicksand. The whole nation of Israel was being pulled down into it, and they were dragging Moses with them. Moses said to God, "If this is the way you will deal with me, then please do me the favor of killing me at once so that I need no longer face this distress." Have you ever had such a notion?

Moses was being ripped apart. He was being torn in two by a stubborn people who refused to let go of the past and take even one leap of faith toward the future. A leap of faith is risky and across uncharted territory, yet a leap of faith is the only way. God will neither surrender the grand future nor let the people slide back into their miserable past. *And there we are.* We are right there—sick to death of manna—we want something to change. Each day is the same. Day after day and week after week, we forge through another day, absolutely sick to death of our very existence. Yet sometimes what we think we need isn't what we need at all.

God knows what we need—harmony in our lives, peace in our hearts, and contentment. Believe me, it comes. It comes from God—through God's will, in God's way, and in God's time. God conquers despair by filling our hearts and minds with the best manna of all—the power of the Holy Spirit. With the Holy Spirit, the future will look brighter. You must know God's glory is upon you. You are journeying to the promised land, the land of hope and freedom. God's plan always makes the situation better, but to live the plan takes a leap of faith. You may be in insurmountable distress and unable to see a way out, but you must let the Holy Spirit carry you through the struggle so you can move toward the vision God clearly has for you.

The story of the Israelites, who are frustrated beyond belief with the bland answer to their hunger—manna—in the wilderness can be read in Numbers 11:1-15. It took the Israelites years to reach the land promised to them by God. But as you will read in Numbers, God did change things for them in God's time. God pulled them out of the unpleasant present, helped them put their miserable past into perspective, and brought them to a new future. It takes time, and waiting for something to change—anything at all—takes a leap of faith and turning all your miserable past and unpleasant present situations over to God. The Holy Spirit will empower you to push forward and out of your despair, depression, and misery. Hang in there.

32

We Are All Dead Ducks

"But who can detect their errors? Clear me from hidden faults" (Psalm 19:12).

Jesus said, "Two men went up to the temple to pray; one of them was a Pharisee and the other was a tax collector." You must remember that a tax collector was a crook—a person who was a Jew but worked for the Roman government. He had a franchise—an area in which he was entitled to collect taxes—and he was told by the Romans what he owed them. Anything else he made over and above that went into his pocket. The tax collectors were despised as turncoats. The other character in Jesus' story, the Pharisee, was one of the most respected people in Judaism of his time. The Pharisee stood by himself and prayed, "God, I thank you that I am not like other people. I am not a thief. I am not a rogue. I am not an adulterer. I am certainly not like this tax collector over here. I fast twice a week. I give away a tenth of my income." That was his speech. He went on interminably like that.

Then the tax collector said (without looking up to the heaven; he looked at his feet), "God be merciful to me, a sinner."

Then Jesus said, "I tell you this man (the tax collector) went to his house justified rather than the other (the Pharisee), for all who exalt themselves will be humbled and all who humble themselves will be exalted."

That is the story. Like all of Jesus' parables, it should carry a warning, which is "this will be hazardous to all your previous opinions about how religion works and how God works." Jesus' parables are designed to outrage and shock the hearers and to show how God has stood almost all of our values on their heads. What this parable is about is not, as it seems to say at the end, the virtue of humility.

The Pharisee's problem was not that he was showing off. It was that he really believed that his stack of good deeds was enough to save him. He believed it was enough—if only everyone else would do what he did; that would be enough to save the whole world.

What God really says in Christ is that human goodness isn't good enough to save us. Human goodness cannot reconcile the world. Basically, if the world could have been reconciled by good advice from God to which human goodness would respond, the world's problems would have been solved ten minutes after Moses got down to the bottom of the mountain with the commandments. Everyone would have read the commandments and said, "Oh, yes, of course," and the problem would have been over. But the world is not saved by good behavior.

The Pharisee's goodness is irrelevant. The tax collector who simply looks at his feet and says "I'm no good" is justified. The point is that both the Pharisee and the tax collector are dead ducks and can do nothing to save themselves. The Pharisee is a very high-class kind of dead duck, but they are both dead as far as being able to reconcile with God. Reconciliation with God is through Jesus' death and resurrection. Jesus did not come to teach the teachable, improve the improvable, or to reform the reform-able. Jesus came to raise the dead—you in your deadness, the Pharisee in his deadness, and the tax collector in his deadness.

However, this parable violates every sense you and I have about the fact that we are basically doing fairly well. If only other people were as nice and considerate and as wonderful as we are, the world would be a better place to live in. God says, "No. That will not work. "The world cannot run that way. It can't be run by people who think they are winners. It can only be run by people who are willing to admit they are losers, for only God has the gift of reconciliation with God.

You still may not like that, because the terrible tax collector—who is really a monstrous character—probably rubs salt in everybody's wounds. He drives around in a stretch limo with a case of Chivas Regal in the back of the trunk and several very expensive call girls with him at all times. He has just been skimming the cream off his neighbor's milk money. The point is that the Pharisee is no less dead than that dreadful character.

What God says is, "I don't care that you are not okay. I will raise you from the death of your lack of okay-ness. I will raise you up. Just admit you are no good, and trust me. All you have to do is recognize that death is the key to your salvation."

The tax collector goes home justified. Let's say he comes back a week later, but nothing has changed. He drives up in the same stretch limo with the same girls in the back and the same expensive scotch. He comes in, and he goes through the same routine. He looks at his feet and says, "God, be merciful to me. I am no good."

What will God say to him? Well, in the way Jesus told the parable, God will say the same thing He said the week before. He will say, "This man goes home justified because he admits he is dead." God didn't tell him the first week, "You are justified, but don't do it again." God said, "I have raised you from your death. You trust that. All right. Go in peace." The second week, there are no changes—the same thing. Do you like that version of the story? No. You don't like that. The rat is getting away with murder.

I'll give you yet another version. Bring the tax collector back the third week for another trip to the temple—but this week, bring him back with some changes in his life. That is what you are itching for—that he has changed or mended his ways, even if just a little. This time he is not driving a stretch limo. He is driving a Hyundai. He only has one girl in the car with him, and he is drinking cheaper scotch and giving the difference to the Heart Fund. Would this make a difference to God? God wasn't interested in the Pharisee's list of really respectable virtues—a really solid citizen—so what makes you think minor improvements in the tax collector win God's favor?

The answer is that *we fear salvation that is so cheap that it saves everyone.* That is where God works. God works in the losers of the world. He works in all of us. What it means—the reason we fear cheap salvation so much—is that in the long run, death gets us all. If death is the only ticket anyone needs to the reconciliation in Jesus and everybody has that ticket, then God has no taste. God is vulgar. God is indiscriminate. God is immoral. God lets in me. God lets in you. All we have to do is believe it, not earn it. Paul writes in Romans, "There is, therefore, now no condemnation to those who are in Christ Jesus."

This parable is about death, and it is about the resurrection from the dead. The point is that *death is all of the resurrection that we can know now.* The most important thing is that we believe in Jesus. The dead will hear the voice of the Son of God, and they will live. I simply trust Jesus will deliver me as he himself rose from the dead. Whatever that means and however it works, I trust Christ, because in His death is my reconciliation, and in my reconciliation is my joy in Him.

33

Jesus Has Your Back

Christ's prayer for his disciples:

I have made your name known to those whom you gave me from the world. They were yours, and you gave them to me; and they have kept your word. Now they know that everything you have given me is from you; for the words that you gave to me I have given to them, and they have received them and know in truth that I came from you; and they believed that you sent me. I am asking on their behalf; I am not asking on behalf of the world, but on behalf of those whom you gave me, because they are yours. All mine are yours, and yours are mine; and I have been glorified in them. And now I am no longer in the world, but they are in the world, and I am coming to you. Holy Father, protect them in your name that you have given me, so that they may be one, as we are one (John 17:6-11).

This message is about keeping another's best interest at heart. Jesus' best interest for each of you is to have a worry-free life. Why? To free you up—to give you the time and space you need to share the gospel. Jesus also knows what is in the best interest for each of us individually. For instance, you may need patience and understanding for the best interest of your child, courage in the face of calamity, or a strong faith while waiting for the perfect answer to a medical diagnoses.

Jesus knows what is in our best interest. The gospel today—often called the high priestly prayer of Jesus—covers many great points and is a deep and necessary study for all Christians. In the last part of the prayer, Jesus speaks about us and the need for God the Father to have our best interest at heart. This prayer of Jesus is just before Gethsemane and Jesus' heart-wrenching, "Father, please take this cup from me" prayer.

Jesus lived in a poor society. At the top of the heap were the Pharisees, and although they counted as only 5-10 percent of the population, they were able to throw around their own best interest and live for their own personal gain. They truly believed they had a hold on God and that the way of the law was theirs to uphold. Jesus entered the scene and challenged their way of life, moving self-interest to interest in another.

The society we live in persuades us to think about ourselves most of the time. The enormous challenge for us is to be contrary to societal teaching. We are to imitate Jesus, and Jesus makes it clear we should have others' best interest at heart.

In three short years Jesus—against all odds—needed to change thinking. He was here to change our response to other people. We live in a "take care of yourself first" society. We are taught to be competitive, selfish, and success-driven. The trouble with competition is that where there is a winner, there is also a loser. We are encouraged to be on the top of the heap, throw around our own best interest, and live by our own agenda. Society teaches us to live for personal gain and personal satisfaction and to be selfish and self-centered. As always, Jesus teaches, demonstrates, and lives the opposite of societal dictates. And we are called to imitate Jesus.

As a mother has the best interest of her child at heart, the husband has his spouse's best interest at heart and a teacher has the dutiful task of teaching our children, having their best interests at heart. We are called to have others' best interest in mind, even though we may not care much for them.

On Memorial weekend, the Iowa Donors Network with the Lion's Eye Bank had a ceremony and dedication service in Iowa City at the Healing Gardens. At the main entrance of the university hospitals, which is a large circular drive, is a circle, and in the middle of this circle is a beautiful garden with trees, flowers, pathways, and streams of water.

The ceremony was well-planned. Tents were up, chairs were generously spaced in different areas for some privacy, there was an elevated platform for speakers, and a vocal group from the hospital sang. Those in attendance were chaplains, doctors, donors' families, and recipients and their families. This was an every-age, every-race gathering for the purpose of the best interest of others.

One speaker was a young man whose life was renewed by his mother, for she gave him one of her kidneys. One speaker was a man who at the age of eighteen was in a farm accident with anhydrous ammonia, which blinded him. Over the next several years, he received cornea transplants, but his body rejected them. A new transplantation procedure was developed in 2009 by a doctor at the University hospitals, and this patient was personally called to come and try this new procedure. He did, and his vision was restored to 20/20. This man's comment was, "I saw my wife for the first time."

Through the unselfish acts of donors and donors' families and the laborious work, study, and ingenuity of a doctor and a team of scientists, a new procedure was developed for the best interest of others. There are people in our lives who demonstrate unselfish acts such as these. We are called to be these people who demonstrate unselfish acts. We may not develop a new medical procedure; however, we are given what we need, as God provides our individual needs. It is vital that we recognize the vast difference between unity, as observed at this wonderful ceremony, and uniformity. Unity is in the best demonstrated in diversity; uniformity is threatened by diversity.

Our Lord chose as disciples men who were radically different in temperament, personality, and political philosophy. It was because of their glaring differences that their unity was so evident. Jesus taught them that the best interest of others did not have limits.

Paul teaches us in 1 Corinthians a good example of how this works. Paul teaches that diversity is not opposed to unity; it is essential to it. How could the body function rightly if every member were an eye or an ear or a mouth? True unity demands diversity, and diversity displays true unity. This is why the prayer of Jesus is so vital for each of us. Jesus prays for the best interest of each of us individually to free us uphold the best interest of others and through this proclaim the gospel of our Lord Jesus Christ.

The movie *Titanic* showed a very excellent depiction of unselfishness and also extreme self-interest. Some people literally fought for a place on the lifeboats, of which there were not enough for each passenger. Other people helped others get into the lifeboats. Honestly, we are in both positions over a lifetime. There are times we need someone to help us into a lifeboat; there are other times we help the other person into the lifeboat.

Tending to others, making necessary sacrifices, giving up our way for others, moving outside the box, and thinking about others' best interests is what we are called to do.

For Jesus, you see, *we* are the other. We are the ones whose best interests are at heart. Jesus has each of our own individual best interests in mind at all times. Our own best interest is to be best we can be. This frees us up to have the best interests of others on our hearts and to proclaim the gospel.

Jesus was soon to leave earth to ascend to the Father's right hand. He needed to leave his life's work—a life lived for each of us—to a small group of disciples. So Jesus prayed. Jesus prayed for the disciples. Jesus prayed for you and me. Jesus prayed for the Father to take care of us, have each of our best interests at heart, and instill in us what is most necessary to free us up to respond to the gospel through proclamation and unselfish care for other people.

As Jesus faced death, he thought of us. As Jesus faced a cruel death, he prayed for our best interest. As Jesus faced death on a cross, his prayer for us was not mere wishful thinking; it was seriously necessary for the good news of Jesus Christ to reach every man, woman, and child through us. This message is about keeping another's best interest at heart.

Thank you, Lord Jesus Christ, for loving us with the power
of the triune God—the Father, Son, and Holy Spirit.
Amen.

Part 7

34

Beneath a Fertile Sky

"Sing to the Lord a new song for he has done marvelous things" (Psalm 98:1)

It has been imperative for me to get out the word about depression being a malady worthy of recognition by all people and especially the church. Depression leaves a lasting imprint on the person who has suffered with and from its devastating symptoms. Depression is no laughing matter. The stigma associated with depression comes in the form of ridicule, indifference, and even contempt.

Hopefully this book offers words of encouragement, hope, and prayers to speak words where you have none left. My goal is to find something—a nugget, some phrase, some particular word—which touches you in your situation. Depression can materialize into something very evil and menacing if left to its own wanderings and its own devices. Seek help if you are depressed.

For me, the blackbird symbolizes the possibility that depression is lurking in the background. The blackbird is a very real depiction of the threat I feel. A friend of mine who suffers with depression refers to it as a black dog following her around. You probably have your own symbolism or aura to give the depression an objective name, for it helps to get it out of a completely subjective mindset.

Remember, depression is a real diagnoses and a real deal; it is not imagined or something you can click off. Developing coping mechanisms is vital—some come naturally; others are self-taught. It is natural to cocoon in; meditation is self-taught.

Many things can help, such as medications prescribed by your doctor; good nutrition; strong support; and the setting of small, attainable goals for yourself, such as brushing your teeth. Christ is with you all the way, comforting you, encouraging you, and telling you are worthwhile and important. Depression is not a sin. It is not your fault. You are not hopeless; it does not last forever, and it is nothing to be ashamed of. God intervenes and is constant during your pain and desperation, sadness and disconnect, fear and loss, despair and grief, and God is with you in your anger.

Anger shows up for various reasons. I was angry about the inability to hold a job, because somewhere in the course of time, depression deemed me unreliable. This attacked our family's financial security and my personal credibility. Faith, trust, and belief in God will see you through the toughest of times, yet the losses are real and life-changing. The Bible can help, for biblical text is alive—the living Word. For that reason, it can buoy you up and help diminish your fears. Verses from the Bible are scattered through this writing to offer you a quick touch of love and security.

Depression comes with decreased energy and chronic exhaustion. It can leave you sensitive to light, sound, and the whole of your environment. It threatens your ability to trust God, revere life, and line up the courage needed to ward off its effects on the self. Depression can become so severe it attacks the very holiness of your being.

It is vitally important to develop strong relationships with other people while you are well so that you have a network of friends and family to rely on when you are sick. You need people who you can call on to drive you places, run errands for you, or call any time. You need someone who doesn't ask many questions, and you must have someone you trust to make some decisions for you. Most of all, you must keep your communication with God open and active. Getting caught up in yourself is natural. Something which can help is to push yourself to pray for other people and always be aware of the world of pain and suffering.

35

Let Us Pray

Lord, enfold me in your arms as Mary enfolded Jesus. Assure me of your presence. Fill me with your Holy Spirit so I may courageously face the truth of who I am and more courageously face the truth of who you would have me be. Help me and all who hear your Word to listen to the prophets of today that we may be changed by your love and empowered to seek out the lost, the lonely, and all who live apart from your love. In Jesus' name we pray. Amen.

36

Save Yourself?

The number of troubled people in congregations is as numerous as the roll call and as plentiful as the professional roster. Some individuals quickly muster up every ounce of courage to rap on the pastor's door as they bring along deep hurt and pain. In all instances, these persons require a bonding empathy with the pastor and need to be reminded of how much God loves them and desires healing and wholeness in their lives. As pastors evaluate the situation, they ask themselves pertinent questions: are this person's needs within the realm of pastoral care? Does this person require further meetings with the pastor or a referral to an appropriate resource? Is this person safe in the time between visits?

Never should someone in depressive trouble be rejected, be told to leave, or have the clergy walk away from them. However, I have found pastors subtly say "save yourself" to the depressed all the time. I am not implying that pastors are totally cold stones, but I am saying pastors leave the depressed in the realm of "save yourself" more often than not. In my experience, pastors live within the assumption that each person has a networking support system that meets his or her individual needs. If there is no support system in place, a pastor must assist the depressed with diligence to help set up adequate networking. It is not the position of the pastor to be all things to everyone, and in the realm of someone's depression, direct contact and support for the depressed must be in place. But I am not sure pastors know if the depressed have a network of support. The assumption is that each person takes care of his or her own troubles with the system each has in place. It is from this premise that pastors often give the message, "You know I care about you, and I hope you are getting the help you need." In other words, "Save yourself."

When pastors visit with a troubled person, do they ask if this is within the realm of pastoral care and who is providing this care? Does this person require a referral to an appropriate resource? Is this referral in place? Is he or she safe in the time between visits?

Pastors not only subtly and not-so-subtly turn the depressed away, but also turn on themselves. If depression hits (if it is even recognized), it is often dismissed as a job hazard. The "save yourself" method will fail. No matter how strong our human will and desire is, saving yourself will not be successful, for to dabble in the very prospect of saving yourself becomes very messy indeed. I speak about this firsthand.

If you are like me, you may figure that all this networking doesn't take place until after disaster hits. Now here I am, as you may be, hanging on to a thin thread with little energy to analyze my surroundings. Making mistakes for the sake of survival is commonplace. So don't beat yourself up if you do not have support right now—but you must take the effort to tune in with someone. You will not get through this depression alone.

As an addendum to losing my job, it must be said that stress is alive and well. If you are an employer, consider this: stress is not your employee's inability to cope; stress is a consequence of the employer's failure to provide a safe system in which to work. If indeed you are the employee, excessive workloads and unreasonable demands are stress-producers, and stress is a bed partner with depression.

37

"Follow Me"

Matthew dropped what he was doing and followed Jesus. This all seems very straightforward, and we have always taken these verses as they stand. "Follow me." It makes a great vision—Jesus came by a complete stranger and said the words, "Follow me." Matthew left behind his tax booth and moved on. Why did he follow Jesus? Matthew was collecting money; why did he give it up to follow some stranger who passed by? Maybe the world of money was getting boring; maybe the world was getting to be too much of a burden—whatever the reason, Matthew chose to follow Jesus, and people have been following Jesus ever since. If Matthew's previous life was fulfilling—if his life had meaning and his life made a positive influence on people—why did he leave it behind? This may be the reason he did follow Jesus—his present life was not fulfilling, and his life had no meaning, for he only made a negative impact on people. Maybe he wanted something better—something different.

How many requests to "follow me" do we receive during a lifetime? Think of all the requests you have followed. Have you followed money around or the urge to steal, drink, or chase around a lie, an empty promise, or a negative life? The strongest "follow me" could be adultery, swindling, having fancy stuff you can't afford, or maybe drugs. But when Jesus comes along and says, "Follow me," how many times do we say, "Not now; maybe later"?

In all our lives, something calls to us, and we don't always answer Jesus. Yet we think of the story of Matthew as a blessed event. Jesus walked by, and Matthew said to himself, "Finally, this is the real thing." He left his troubled life behind and followed Jesus. The problem with this is that Matthew didn't get everything right. Matthew didn't fall into instant sainthood. Matthew's decision to follow Jesus was because of Jesus. Jesus was the difference, not Matthew's response. Jesus makes the difference in our life's choices too.

So how do we know the difference? How do we know if it is friendly Jesus calling our name? There are only two answers here—it is either Jesus or it is not. There is no gray area. How do we know? We know when we cross our forehead in the name of the triune God; say "I am a baptized child of God"; pick up the Bible and read it, for the words of the Lord are life-giving; and pray "God help me" and God is ever-faithful. But you may say, "There are times I have called to God and heard nothing." Is that true? Does God absent God's self from us? The answer is *no.* God is always present in our every breath; the grace of God never leaves us.

The words Jesus said to Matthew—"follow me"—Jesus says to us every day. Now we may go off searching for Jesus all we want. You have heard the question, "Have you found your personal Savior?" or "Have you found Jesus?" I am here to tell you that Jesus was never lost. *You* might be lost from time to time, but Jesus is always there saying, "Follow me." Following may not always be what we want—it may get messy—but it will fulfill you. It will give your life meaning. You will dine with the despised and defend the oppressed. You will use Jesus' Word for good.

All it takes to leave behind the clutches of the world are the words of Jesus: "Follow me." You are reoriented to Jesus and your real self daily. The more you are tempted, the more you must pray, read the Bible, and follow Jesus. The more you pray, read the Bible, and follow Jesus, the more you will be tempted. But Jesus is the way, the truth, and the only life. Jesus says to us daily, "Follow me."

"If the Lord is God follow him" (1 Kings 18:21b).

"The Lord is my shepherd . . . surely goodness and mercy shall follow me" (Psalm 23:1a, 6a).

"And immediately they left their nets and followed him" (Mark 1:18).

"Then he said to them all, 'If any want to become my followers, let them deny themselves and take up their cross daily and follow me'" (Luke 9:23).

"My sheep hear my voice, I know them and they follow me" (John 10:27).

"These follow the lamb wherever he goes" (Revelation 14:4).

Part 8

38

The Holy Spirit Intercedes for Us

The assurance that the Spirit intercedes for us affords us the opportunity to wait patiently, for our hope is in the Spirit. The truth is that we cannot escape the labor pains, but we do not suffer alone, for the Spirit is always with us, interceding on our behalf. With this hope we were saved; we are saved by hope, in hope, to hope, for hope. Even though our sighs baffle words, we live in the ongoing action of the communal celebration of the victory of Jesus Christ. Romans 8:22-27 speaks this for us:

We know that the whole creation has been groaning in labor pains until now; and not only the creation; but we ourselves, who have the first fruits of the Spirit, groan inwardly while we wait for adoption, the redemption of our bodies. For in hope we were saved. Now hope that is seen is not hope. For who hopes for what is seen? But if we hope for what we do not see, we wait for it with patience. Likewise the Spirit helps us in our weakness; for we do not know how to pray as we ought, but that very Spirit intercedes with signs too deep for words. and God, who searches the heart, knows what is the mind of the Spirit, because the Spirit intercedes for the saints according to the will of God.

39

The Tides Have Shifted

The question has changed from asking myself how to stay alive in the physical sense—meaning no more suicidal thoughts—to how to stay alive in the emotional sense. Life—whatever that may be—is put out to drift for a quite a long time when you are depressed, for only the motions of moving through the day without enthusiasm or desire are present, and the movement toward healing, wholeness, or any semblance of wellness is very gradual. Yes, it is all connected. The physical, emotional, mental, psychological, and spiritual all are connected, but without some physical life, face it—the rest are dead, too. Once the decision to stay alive becomes stronger than the sharks trying to kill you off and the rescue boat picks you up, physical safety can be reality again. It is time to work on the wellness of the spirit. I

In a real survival situation, you stare death in the face. If you look away, you will lose. I have found there is only one thing more despairing than looking death in the face, and that is looking life in the face. The emotional drain of staying physically alive comes from a deep innate response focused on self-preservation. Now that you have made the decision to stay physically alive, you face the challenge of staying emotionally alive.

You know physical life, because when the rescue team comes and pulls you out of the dark and throws you into the boat, you hear people speaking, "Are you okay?" "Get her warmed up." "Start rubbing her feet; get some circulation going." "Put on the chicken soup; we've got a live one here." But being in the drowning mode of the emotional or mental kind doesn't draw attention on its own. No one comes with a life boat now, as sick as you are. Swim, baby, swim—and hope you are swimming in the right direction.

Laurence Gonzales says, "Primary emotions are the ones you're born with, such as the drive to obtain food or the reaction of reaching out to grab something if you feel yourself falling." The trick is that you need something or someone to grab hold of, and you can't take for granted that what or who you think will be there as you are grabbing will grab back. You must get your grabbers in place when you are well. The big problem with this is when I am well, I can't stand the thought of being sick again, and preparing for it by trimming the sails and fixing the nets seems to invite trouble. But I have yet to find any other way to go about staying alive other than to plan for disaster before it pounds you to death.

Let me offer an example. A colleague of mine—one with whom I have shared much of my story and who herself has emotional turmoil from time to time—by all appearances seems a person I would be able to grab for if I was going down for the count, but I never asked her. I assumed she would be there, which was the wrong assumption. She wasn't able to grab back. There are a few reasons she could not grab me: she didn't have much of a grip on herself, and this colleague couldn't help, because she wasn't able to read my outward actions.

These are good points to think about, because we have a tendency to gravitate to like-minded people, but that doesn't necessarily mean they can help when the going gets tough. They may understand your desperate situation, but they can't always help. This is no fault of theirs, but if you have similar pains as someone else, you cannot assume they will react in the same way you would react. Thus it is imperative that you explicitly communicate with your confidants.

When I am in the throes of disaster and talking to a confidant, I will often make fun of my own dilemma, laughing and chiding myself. Even in the worst of situations, I may continue to laugh. This hysteria can be the only way I can deal with the reality of my pain. Like the old adage says, "If I don't laugh, I'll cry." My colleague reads this the way she sees it—I was laughing, thus I must have been fine with what was going on in my life. From all outward appearances, it was just that—laughing—but it was an inside hysteria.

Something else to keep in mind is that just because you say something, it doesn't mean the person you are talking to will get it. This same colleague said to me after I had a major fall, "You said you were desperate, but you didn't sound desperate." This one statement has run through my mind a million times, for I have tried to decipher it, and I come up blank. The closest I can think is that if I were to say to you, "I'd rather be dead," your thoughts might run like this: *she'd rather be dead than wear orange; she'd rather be dead than return to the afternoon lecture.* I just didn't give her enough information to go on, and I expected her to pick it up and translate the end of the thought for me. What I was saying was, "I'd rather be dead than to face one more horrible night like last night." Now at least I have given her something to look at more objectively.

An excellent way to throw yourself some tidbits to keep afloat is to promise yourself something for later, such as, "When I'm done with this chapter, I can have a bagel." It provides a commitment to the bagel. You have a future—a place in the world in a time that has not yet come. When you are very sick, reward yourself with small stitches of time where you declare breath—just breath.

The safety zone from avoiding physical harm to making progress to healing the emotional self may still be in the distance; however, being turned around and headed in the right direction is great progress. The trip to the epicenter of depression and despair is behind you; the greatest hurt will leave you alone for a while. It is time to use all your fear and pain to your advantage and to let it buoy you up. Being on the other side of the boundary line means you must learn to adapt. There is no model for living here, and there is no normal adaptation to the environment for us to observe or to learn from. We are on our own.

Each motion within emotional wellness will need to be thought through with the steps laid out in sequence. Just as you must go through the steps of brushing your teeth, you will need to go through the steps of having a happy thought. Since sequencing our steps toward emotional health is not a prepared journey—there's no Mapquest available—we are going to have to do the best with what we've got. As we set out on this journey to a new place of emotional safety, the map will be drawn as we go. There will be landmarks along the way—things that are recognizable—but it is important to know where you are starting.

Earlier I had to admit I was lost—totally and completely lost. I was in a space and place with no direction or compass, no way out, and no mind-map of entry or exit. Being in that place not only removes any sense of direction, but also destroys all known landmarks. Depression is like having no self. It is absolutely impossible to make any move out of the hideous hole when you don't exist, for depression removes your very existence. To expect much traveling or journey from yourself isn't feasible. You must rely on innate homing devices. This depression that plagues has a strong homing device which in psychological terms is called agoraphobia—simply put, the fear to leave home. Well, it all makes perfect sense, really, because having depression is being lost, and I am the least lost at home—so why would I want to leave this place and be overwhelmed even more besides already being lost? Home offers objective landmarks, because home is familiar with few surprises and no major decisions to make. Home provides safety. My husband, Rich, would at times say to me, "Come on, we need to get you out of here." That worked for me, because *we* were leaving the house.

Being lost requires a new way of looking ahead, because the old map is gone. The map of emotional movement to wellness can only be developed if you admit you are lost, resign yourself to the plight of being lost, and make a commitment to find yourself. Depression is like going through your own death, thus there is the need to grieve your own loss. The stages of denial, anger, bargaining, and acceptance are all in the death of spirit by the hands of depression.

Our real environment has changed. We are starting from a brand new spot. This is where apathy can set in and lead to a complete deterioration of the psychic, so take time to rest, eat right, pray, and meditate. We didn't get sick overnight, and we are not going to get well overnight either.

Fatigue must be considered yet again. Fatigue is not only a physical condition, but also the overwhelming exhaustion of psychological distress. I have found it essential to not let fatigue set in and take over, because it causes me immeasurable setbacks. Once real fatigue sets in, it can be almost impossible to wiggle out from under its weight. Fatigue is not just a matter of being physically tired, but also a psychological deprivation and a true spiritual collapse.

Writing all this down allows me to get better. It helps me to ensure my own survival, and helping you takes me out of myself. Writing helps me rise above my own fears and moves me from being the victim to being on the rescue team. By writing about this life of depression, clarity of thought, perseverance to press on, and most of all, the feeling that you are with me and I am not alone come to me.

40

The Change with Each Season

*"And those who know your name put their trust in you,
for you O Lord have not forsaken those who seek you"
(Psalm 9:10).*

Each season comes with its own set of challenges. I have found it necessary to be prepared and not let each seasonal change catch me by surprise, for it will generally throw me into a tail spin. Reminding myself of the goodness of each season rather than bemoaning it can help me keep my nose out of the water of depression. This is a list of words I relate to the seasons.

Winter	Spring	Summer	Fall
Long nights	Flowers	Long days	Football
Despair	Lent	Vacation	Leaves
Depression	Easter	Swimming	Crisp air
Serious	Graduations	Family	Putting away
Christmas	Rain	Camping	Storing up
Winter solstice	Green	Nature	School
Stress	Celebration	Busy	Birthdays
Frenzy	Music	Campfires	Thanksgiving

Cold and snow	New birth	Jovial	Campfires
Lonely	Mud	Happiness	Work
Melancholy	Cleaning	Gleeful	Anxiety
Anxiety	Yard	Relax	Cozy

I try really hard to bring the goodness of my favorite seasons into my least favorite seasons. For instance, I love sunshine, swimming, and camping. In the winter, I try to go swimming and get some rays in a tanning bed.

The hardest time of the year for many people is winter. Advent can be especially hard with the frenzy of Christmas preparations adding to an already busy schedule. A special service called Blue Advent is one I found helpful. It allows me to feel what I need to feel during Advent rather than trying faux cheer.

41

Blue Advent

Read Job 6. We admit we are powerless, and parts of our life are out of our control and unmanageable. There are times when we are confused and overwhelmed by the pain in our lives that we wish we could disappear. No matter what we do, we are powerless to change things for the better. The weight of the pain and sadness seems too heavy to bear. We can't see why our hearts don't just break—or maybe they have. Job felt that way. He'd lost everything, even though he loved and believed in God. His ten children were dead, and he had lost his business, riches, and health all in a matter of days. It is said he was left with a sharp-tongued wife and three friends who blamed him for his own situation.

Job cried out Job 6:2, "If my sadness could be weighted and my troubles be put to the scales, they would be heavier than all the sands of the sea." Job went on to say, "Oh that I might have my request, that god would grant my hope. I wish God would crush me. I wish God would reach out his hand and snuffed me out." In other words, Job was saying, "I do not have the strength to endure; I do not have a goal that encourages me to carry on. I am utterly helpless without any chance of success."

Have you ever felt utterly helpless? Even though we are pressed to the end point, there is still hope that our lives will change—that things will change. Life can be good again. Whether we suffer from physical pain, emotional pain, the loss of a spouse, a disappointing career, divorce, loneliness, depression, or addiction, often the nights are long and difficult. At least during the daylight hours, our work or other activities can help take our minds off our situation.

When night falls and we are alone, the reality of our pain stares us in the face with no distractions. It is then that we can talk to God about our pain. God will listen, and God will comfort. We are never alone; we can always talk to God. Even though Job was in anguish, he recognized that God was the only one who could take away the pain. God is there to comfort us. God's timing may not be what we could consider ideal, but God's perspective and timing are always the best. We can trust God to rescue us—but in God's time, not ours.

Only God truly knows and understands our circumstances. Sometimes we may feel God is unfair. Recall that God is merciful, and it is by grace that we do not receive what we deserve! When we feel that God isn't being fair, we should remember that if God were fair, we would never be able to enter his presence. When God is unfair, it is always on the side of mercy.

Job lamented the absence of a mediator to stand between himself and God. We need not make that same plea, for God has sent a mediator in Jesus Christ. We can take our cases directly to God, because Jesus' death gave us access to God's presence. When we feel as if we cannot stand any more pain, we can go to Jesus with our request for peace. He will listen to us and answer our prayers. Although God might not answer our prayers the way we think he should, God is perfect, and perfect peace comes in God's time.

Jesus assured us that we have a place with him in eternity. He gave us a picture of hope that we could hold on to in our grief. When we suffer, sometimes hope seems far away. Maybe like Job, we can't imagine a future of light when feeling enveloped in darkness. But we can hope. We have Jesus' promise, and God is sovereign indeed. Just as Job was trying to make sense of his suffering, so do we. As we devote our hearts to God, we deepen our relationship with God. But this fellowship with God doesn't eliminate all our suffering. Pain is part of life, whether we are close to God or not. Our hope is in eternity with Christ.

In the midst of Job's suffering, he said, How frail is humanity, how short is life, and how full of trouble, like a flower, we blossom for a moment and then wither. Like the shadow of a passing cloud, we quickly disappear." God alone knows and understands all this. Life brings hurts, and there are no guarantees that we will escape them. But through suffering, we can learn to live by faith rather than by our own strength. We can learn that even when suffering leads to doubt, God is still with us.

42

Lenten Discipline

Remember that the very disciples who ran and hid when Jesus was arrested became fearless in the face of death after receiving the peace Jesus brought to them.

Each Lenten season brings a challenge for me. During this somber season of the church year during an already dreary winter, it is hard to keep positive. If I approach each Lenten season as the opportunity to try something new in the form of Christian discipline, I have something positive to focus on during this time. Rather than feeling a sense of sacrifice, it is better to consider adding something positive to my life. Rather than a personal discipline, consider a relational discipline. Spend more time at night putting the children to bed with a good Bible story, set aside time each week to invite someone over to eat or go out for coffee, or offer more phone calls to friends and family.

Part 9

43

A Responsive Litany

Jesus said, "I am the light of the world. Whoever follows me will never walk in darkness but will have the light of life.

Come, let us turn to the Lord, that he may teach us to pray and that we may walk in his paths.

"I will lead the blind by a road they do not know. I will turn the darkness before them into light."

You show me the path of life. In your presence, there is fullness of joy; in your right hand are pleasures forevermore.

"My sheep hear my voice. I know them, and they follow me."

He leads me in the paths of righteousness for his name's sake.

"Do not fear, for I am with you; do not be afraid, for I am your God.

I will strengthen you, I will help you, and I will uphold you with my victorious right hand."

Oh, send out your light and your truth; let them lead me. In the path of your judgments, O Lord, we wait for you.

44

Devotion

Devotions are very important to maintaining equilibrium. Schedule or set aside uninterrupted time for devotions as often as you can. Laying down your burden is very helpful to recovering from depression. Some elements you can have in your devotions are listed here for you.

- Invoke the Holy Spirit to come and be with you.
- Read the Bible.
- Read a printed devotion.
- Pray.
- Praise the Lord through song, poems, or readings.
- Meditate.
- Study a phrase or a word from you readings.
- Offer commemoration to martyrs, saints, or mystics.
- Ponder, consider, contemplate, and think in the now.
- Repent and make confession.
- Reflect on your day.
- Be still and calm.

45

Bible Study

*"Blessed be the god of Shadrach, Meshach and Abednego,
who has sent his angel and delivered his servants who
trusted in him" (Daniel 3:28).*

Bible study is an important piece to maintaining your spiritual health, which influences your entire being: physical, mental, and emotional health. Bible study is the greatest holistic dose of anything you can get. Start always and foremost with biblical study. Bible study is not an attempt to dismantle the story, rearrange it, or pull it apart. Bible study is moving around and through the story without disrupting the story. Looking at a Bible story from different angles helps us see dimensions of the living Word as we live in it. It is more than just the printed word on paper. As we study a passage of Scripture, we enter its space, existence, and the dynamics of the text. Our own relationship with the text becomes stronger, multi-faceted, and enhanced. Just as we spend time with a good friend, the more we learn about him, the more his uniqueness and special qualities shine through. As the weeks and months go by, we come to rely more and more on God, who is revealed to us in our own personal or group Bible study. God moves with us in our space and through our ups and downs of being alive.

The Bible is the living Word of God. It is moving and growing as we move and grow. The stories, messages, and details of the Bible move with us, and as we are in a living relationship with them, they embrace us, comfort us, shake a finger at us, hold us accountable, and challenge us. The living Word of God is a personal relationship between you and God. God wants and desires an open and honest relationship with each one of us. The Bible is one of the ways God wants to be with, speak with, tend to, care for, move with, and grow with us. There are many ways to be with the Bible. We each have our own ways of being with the living Word of God.

We may stroll by the Bible as it sits on the shelf, often intimidated and concerned about what we know or don't know about the Bible, such as the different books of the Bible. Rest assured—we are not expected to know anything. We come as children of God, and while our eyes rest on God, God's eyes certainly rest on us. We may save our study of the Bible for when we are with other people. We may let the pastor lead us through the Bible. The way we come in contact with the Bible isn't the important piece; the important thing is that we do come in contact with the Bible.

Also, the Bible is not the only way to be with God; it is an avenue God has provided for us. Baptism, communion, confession and absolution, worship, and prayer are a few of the other ways God is present with us. The methods of Bible study are extensive; some have fancy names, and some are hundreds to thousands of years old.

Each day, the Bible study and the story it tells us will met our need for the day. We may hear and feel it, but we will know it, for the present time and moment will never again be the same. The living Word lives with and in you. A way to enter the Bible is to enter a story, read through it out loud, and listen to the story. Then read it a second time. Read the text the third time. Each time, move in the text as a participant of the text. Listen to the characters, and put yourself in their shoes. It is quite simple—find a text you want to read with no prerequisite needed, read it aloud, and read it a second and third time, each time entering the text more deeply. That is it, and it will change your life.

46

A Full Life

Jean became an inspiration to me the first time I met her. She had been hospitalized for many days, and each day, her body became more frail. One evening, she was—quite to my surprise—sitting up in a wheelchair, staring at a carton of pudding. She was willing to talk openly about intimate aspects of facing her own imminent death. People with degenerative or terminal illness often withdraw from others; however, she chose to die as she lived—as fully as possible. She became a guide to me. She showed me how to care for the mind and the spirit when the body grows frail. Listening to this fragile woman was uplifting to me. She maintained an alive attitude as she wasted away and neared death. I'm not sure I could face the same thing with such courage. In her last smile and what became her last whispered words to me, she said, "This pudding isn't fit for human consumption."

47

Psalm 121

I look up to the mountains—does my help come from there?

My help comes from the Lord, who made the heavens and the earth!

The Lord will not let me stumble and fall; the Lord watches over me and the Lord will not sleep.

Indeed, the Lord who watches over Israel never tires and never sleeps.

The Lord watches over me!

The Lord stands beside me as a protective shade.

The sun will not hurt me by day, nor the moon at night.

The Lord keeps me from all evil and preserves my life.

The Lord keeps watch over me as I come and go, both now and forever.

Conclusion

Living with Major Depression

Depression can change a good day into a bad day; a once-productive and independent you become unproductive and dependent. There can be control of depression with the right medications and the proper medical care, but regardless of the medication, depression is still a diagnosis without a cure. It is important to realize depression is not your fault, and experiencing it does not mean you are a failure. I was once told that if I had real peace in the Lord, I would not have depression. Truly, this just isn't correct. Christians do get depressed. Because there are physical symptoms with the decrease of serotonin uptake, medications are necessary. Taking meds does not isolate you, and you should not feel guilty for needing medication.

The development of depression is a physical disorder, plus it comes with life's circumstances, historical family makeup, genetics, and major life changes. When you look in the mirror and wonder who you are looking at, you are looking at a child of God created in the image of the living Lord. The more you know about your depression—what triggers it, how to cope with it, which medications work, and which therapist you connect with—the more control you will have so you feel adequate to the condition without attempting to escape to forget or remove the feelings.

Escaping the feelings of depression can come in many ways. I would sleep. There are very dangerous and deadly escape routes—none of which work—such as recreational drug use, alcohol, recreational sexual activity, or spending sprees, with the greatest attempt at escape through suicide. If you have feelings of suicide, call someone immediately. Do no attempt to cover up the feelings; become accountable to another person. Call 911 or a suicide hotline number from your internet. Call your psychiatrist, therapist, doctor, neighbor, or a friend, but connect with someone immediately.

Depression affects each person differently. Depression can surface as a constant threat to life, a gnawing heartache, a continual sense of extreme sadness, a debilitating disease, a curse, and/or a blessing. No one is immune to depression, for there is no shot, dose of sweetness, or special pill that resolves depression completely or keeps it at bay forever. The best we can do is find and accept good medical care, develop and use aggressive coping skills, and release our pain and misery over to Jesus.

Finding and accepting good medical care and therapy is challenging, because it forces us to admit something is wrong and it is something we cannot handle on our own. These thoughts are a detriment to our own recovery and well-being, but the negative stigma connected with depression is societal dictate. The strength to move into the medical system comes from the one who endorses it completely—Jesus. Jesus is for our getting help. Jesus is with us all the way, and Jesus will not disappoint.

There was a time I asked, "Why me? Why do I have to be the one with depression? Why I am the one who has had my life and the life of my family mutilated by such a horrific condition? Why am I the one with this character flaw (as I was taught to think of it)?" First of all, depression is not a character flaw, and second of all, why not me?

Through the course of years spent attempting to get adequate care and finally receiving excellent medical care (thank you, Dr. G.) and the ability to stay strong in my faith, I say thanks be to God. I know some of you have had your very faith totally rattled and shaken by depression. Remember, you are not on a hit list to get depression; you just happen to be the one with depression. Seeking help from the medical profession is necessary, and Jesus wholeheartedly approves, or there wouldn't be so many good psychiatrists in the world.

Hopefully this book has offered you hope and courage—hope that you will come through depression and see the sun again and courage to fight for your life through every means possible.

Why not me? I have learned an immense amount about human nature, the human condition, and human suffering. Most of all, through the years, I have learned of the unwavering and unconditional love God has for me.

My husband had a phrase that helped me out very much, and I still hear it in my heart: "Take care of your-self today, good-lookin'."